Accession no.
36

D1141954

WITHDRAWN

PRAI!

ENLIGHTENED

ORGANIZATION

"Berney bridges multiple disciplines to offer wisdom and clarity into the heart of what matters in business."
Andrew Kakabadse, Professor of Governance and Leadership, Henley Business School

"As organizations and their leaders face more complex challenges, they need new tools. But the tools offered by consultants often fail to connect the organizational challenge to our own lived experience. Catherine Berney's wide-ranging and highly readable book rests on an invaluable insight – the way to understand and meet the needs of organizations is to understand and meet our own needs as human beings. This book can help you become a better leader and a more fulfilled person."
Matthew Taylor, Chief Executive, RSA

"This great book puts the right tools in the hands, minds and hearts of organizations and the people who work within them."
David Lauterstein, Co-founder and Director, Lauterstein-Conway Massage School, Austin, Texas

"Many books have been written on the theory of leadership; this book underlines the need for boards to take some clothes off and really look at the body they are dealing with; not design a strategy that gets a size 20 body into a size 8 Chanel dress without changing diet and exercise...."
Sue O'Brien OBE, CEO, UK, Norman Broadbent

"I like this book. Catherine Berney is a wise and practical companion on the leader's journey. She speaks with equal sense about the individual, about courageous conversations between colleagues, about groups and systems, risks and solutions. This book is built on good theory and will stimulate good practice."
Mark Goyder, Founder Director, Tomorrow's Company

"Although the title says it all, the full understanding of what the author sets forth for us about this new working dynamic and why we seriously need to grasp these concepts became more and more clear with every 'enlightening' chapter."
Carol Vahey, Global Consultant, Head of Talent Development for one of the top global fund management companies

"An essential read for business leaders operating in an increasingly demanding and complicated world. With traditional management strategies less and less relevant, *The Enlightened Organization* provides a set of simple tools to help us navigate this new environment with skill and ease."
Mary Heaney, Director, Futurelex and *The Global Legal Post*

LIS - LIBRARY

Date	Fund
16.5.14	cur -che

Order No.
250 1909

University of Chester

The Enlightened Organization

Executive tools and techniques from the world of organizational psychology

Catherine Berney

BCL, Solicitor, MSc Organizational Psychology, Mediator
Visiting Fellow Cranfield School of Management

KoganPage

LONDON PHILADELPHIA NEW DELHI

Publisher's note

Every possible effort has been made to ensure that the information contained in this book is accurate at the time of going to press, and the publishers and author cannot accept responsibility for any errors or omissions, however caused. No responsibility for loss or damage occasioned to any person acting, or refraining from action, as a result of the material in this publication can be accepted by the editor, the publisher or the author.

First published in Great Britain and the United States in 2014 by Kogan Page Limited

Apart from any fair dealing for the purposes of research or private study, or criticism or review, as permitted under the Copyright, Designs and Patents Act 1988, this publication may only be reproduced, stored or transmitted, in any form or by any means, with the prior permission in writing of the publishers, or in the case of reprographic reproduction in accordance with the terms and licences issued by the CLA. Enquiries concerning reproduction outside these terms should be sent to the publishers at the undermentioned addresses:

2nd Floor, 45 Gee Street	1518 Walnut Street, Suite 1100	4737/23 Ansari Road
London EC1V 3RS	Philadelphia PA 19102	Daryaganj
United Kingdom	USA	New Delhi 110002
		India

www.koganpage.com

© Catherine Berney, 2014

The right of Catherine Berney to be identified as the author of this work has been asserted by her in accordance with the Copyright, Designs and Patents Act 1988.

ISBN   978 0 7494 7027 2
E-ISBN 978 0 7494 7028 9

British Library Cataloguing-in-Publication Data

A CIP record for this book is available from the British Library.

Library of Congress Cataloging-in-Publication Data

Berney, Catherine (Organizational psychologist)
   The enlightened organization: executive tools and techniques from the world of organizational psychology / Catherine Berney.
      pages cm
   Includes index.
   ISBN 978-0-7494-7027-2 – ISBN 978-0-7494-7028-9 (ebk) 1. Organizational behavior.
2. Corporate culture. 3. Organizational effectiveness. I. Title.
   HD58.7.B4645 2014
   658.4001'9–dc23
                                                                                    2013049651

Typeset by Amnet
Print production managed by Jellyfish
Printed and bound by CPI Group (UK) Ltd, Croydon, CR0 4YY

CONTENTS

FOREWORD BY ANDREW KAKABADSE

One of the primary dilemmas for leaders today is how best to operate in an increasingly complex and inter-connected environment which is changing all the time. Hierarchy and known strategies are falling away, being replaced by values, relatedness and emergence. Organizations, and therefore their executive leaders, need increasingly to focus on winning hearts and minds, building radar and reach, maintaining strategic stakeholder relationships, and ultimately protecting fiercely their brand and reputation.

Catherine Berney offers here considerable hope of success in resolving this dilemma. Her enlightened organization:

- defines and embodies its purpose in the world;
- understands and plays to its strengths, while also being attentive to its weaknesses;
- retains an openness and spirit of inquiry about itself, others and its operating environment, remaining always alert to what might be required of it;
- is discerning about the actions to be taken in facing its daily challenges with success.

There have been many recent examples of global organizations in which performance or reputation has suffered as a consequence of being blind to the characteristics of the enlightened organization. Some, for example, forgot purpose and went bankrupt. Others failed to appreciate and develop the skill set required for leading in these changing times. Some were simply not able to adapt, remaining closed and defended, and ultimately lost touch with the market within which they were operating. And many collapsed or lost considerable sums of money, in continuing to pursue needless activities when the figures simply did not add up.

This book offers the executive reader practical models and techniques that will help them to address their own unique dilemmas of leadership on behalf of their organization. Drawing on her background in law, finance and organizational psychology, Catherine Berney bridges multiple disciplines to offer wisdom and clarity into the heart of what matters in business today. She demonstrates how work is required at both the personal and, systemic level if real success or enlightenment is ever to occur; and, in this light, her model of the two-pronged tuning fork suggests resonance, and the ultimate fine tuning of both.

Andrew Kakabadse
Professor of Governance and Leadership
at Henley Business School

ACKNOWLEDGEMENTS

This book would never have happened without the support of so many people; teachers, clients, family and friends.

Professionally, I would like to thank Jacquie Drake, at Cranfield School of Management, for inviting me, over 18 years ago, to work experientially with the most amazing list of clients, from all sectors and all parts of the globe. I would like to acknowledge the influence on my work of the Royal Society for the encouragement of Arts, Manufactures and Commerce, Tomorrow's Company and The Grubb Institute, particularly for the way in which they have enabled me to work more systemically with clients. Finally, I would like to thank John Hurrell from Airmic, for his kindness in allowing me to refer to his research. I have used these case studies throughout the text, rather than many of my own client personal histories, because they are in the public domain and can be followed up in more detail if required.

Personally, you would not be reading this, thankfully edited version, without the wisdom, kindness and encouragement of some dear friends, Helen Kwan, Dina Maguire and Clair Wills, and of course my wonderfully enthusiastic editor, Liz Gooster.

Finally, to my family, without whom I could not have persevered, thank you from the bottom of my heart.

Introduction

If the doors of perception were cleansed every thing would appear to man as it is. Infinite. WILLIAM BLAKE

Wilful blindness is a legal term that refers to the responsibility that a person is deemed to have for things that they might not have known but should have. It was invoked by the judge when convicting Ken Lay and Jeff Skilling in 2006 for their part in the demise of the large US corporation, Enron.

In practice, we are all quite often blind to what is going on within our organizations; especially now, as events seem to be speeding up and complexity and change are becoming the norm. This book lifts a veil so that more of what we choose – at some unconscious level – not to see, can be revealed to us. We can then begin to understand more clearly what is actually going on and how we might, in performing our role, be better able to help.

Organizations form the lifeblood of our society and hold the power to shape and transform our world. They hold the potential, through interconnectedness and creativity, to build something altogether great. This is even more true now, as companies grow in size and extend their reach. But, operating, as they do, within a complex and changing global environment, they need increasingly to be able to respond more effectively if they are to realize their desired impact in the world.

It does, of course, fall on us, as leaders, managers and executives, to do this work of seeing more clearly on our organization's behalf. Yet many of my clients report that they are feeling increasingly confused and anxious about the lack of clarity that they are experiencing in their role. They are being empowered and indeed required to be more accountable for creating the future success of their organizations. Yet they feel more bereft than ever of precedents or guidelines that they can follow in order to achieve this. The old models no longer seem to work or apply.

Like many of them, you may be excited about the enormity of the possibilities that there are now for you to have greater impact within your role. And yet this may also be a slightly overwhelming place from which to operate in practice, as a leader or manager within your business.

Objectives

My objective in writing this book is to help you to navigate your way more skilfully through this changing commercial landscape by helping you to understand what is actually going on within your organization. This is so that you can then flourish and make your rightful contribution at work, while also raising the levels of consciousness and success of your organization. In particular, I will address:

- your purpose and motivation – and that of your organization;
- your strengths and what it is that you can best offer within your role;
- what colleagues and other stakeholders can offer by way of difference to support the whole organization;
- areas where you could develop the potential of yourself and others;
- how to work with the blocks that stop you and others from being great;
- the cultivation of a spirit of inquiry about your role, your organization and the wider system and context within which you operate; and
- ways in which you can ultimately become more discerning and skilful in the actions that you consciously choose to take working to purpose, within your role and on behalf of your organization.

How I can help

In my 20 years of consulting as an organizational psychologist, my role has always been to help people to see more clearly so that they can be the very best that they can be and thereby create a more enlightened organization. I do not subscribe to a 'silver bullet' or 'one size fits all' solution but instead offer an eclectic mix of approaches. These cross different disciplines and bridge the diverse worlds of business and psychology, as well as introducing new ways of thinking about the sciences and our interconnectedness to one another.

The tools and models that I present in this book are the ones that I have found the most helpful when working with clients, as well as on my own personal and professional journey. They are, therefore, the models that I would use with you were I working with you in person. Each of you will be at a different level of transition in your role and facing different and unique challenges. The book offers numerous models and techniques and asks you to choose which of the particular approaches or 'ways in' appeals to you at this moment in time depending on your context.

The two-pronged model

My 'two-pronged' tuning fork approach to realizing the enlightened organization looks at (see Figure 0.1 below):

- the personal and interpersonal in order to see where, in the midst of the endless complexity and change, we might be blocked professionally and creatively and how, in working skilfully with this insight and awareness, we could reclaim and unleash our own purpose, passion and potency; and

- the organization, more broadly, in terms of system and context so that we can understand and see the nature of the water that we are actually swimming in, and therefore make more intelligent choices in stepping forth and shaping our collective business path.

FIGURE 0.1 The two-pronged model

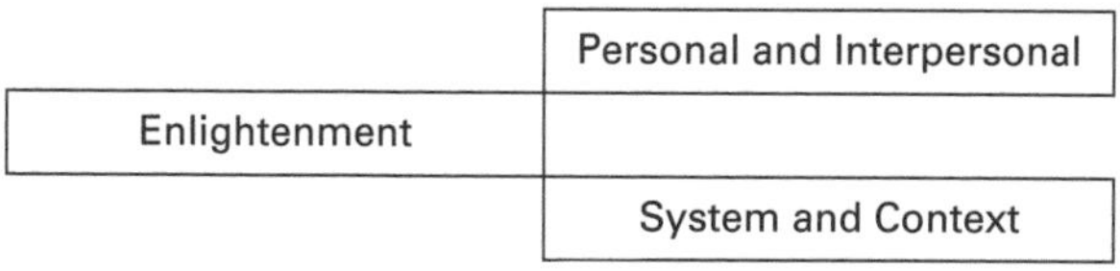

By creating parallel shifts in both prongs we can enable real progress to occur. Then the task is one of balancing and adjusting the elements comprised within each prong so that they resonate and stay attuned with one another.

The choice: To see more clearly and respond

As the song goes, 'The times they are a-changing'. Businesses need to stay in touch and be aware in all sorts of ways if they are to survive and flourish. Increasingly, many organizations see that in order to continue to do business they need to be mindful of how they interact and are perceived within their wider community. Take, for example, the recent pressure on organizations such as Amazon and Starbucks to pay more tax in countries such as the United Kingdom, where they have some of their largest consumer markets. Legally, these companies have been able to structure their global tax arrangements in such a fashion that they have paid relatively little tax to date. But questions have recently been asked about what this attitude communicates in terms of brand. Adverse public opinion has forced these organizations to reconsider their approach, so that they are now volunteering to pay additional amounts of tax in consumer markets such as Ireland and the United Kingdom.

Organizations cannot, of course, read this book nor can they take the first step, but you, the reader, can. The book invites you to become more fully conscious, realizing more about yourself and others in role as well as understanding and appreciating more about system and context in order that you can then create enhanced success for both yourself and your organization in the future.

PART ONE
The issues

Complexity and change

01

Letting go of the illusion of control

...all is flux, all is flow, nothing is permanent... contemplation of impermanence cultivates the capacity to let go of the pictures of the past and future and the illusion of control, and in so doing so foster the capacity to be fully 'present' in the 'present'. SHELLEY OSTROFF

Complexity

Global reach, new technologies, increased mobility and a breakdown in traditional boundaries is making life at work and the world of business increasingly complex, and in a way that affects us all. When I first started out as a young lawyer, I travelled daily to the head office in the city of London, had my own large room that was full of books, pens, paper and a dictation machine, and there was no such thing as working from home. I shared a secretary who had a rather enormous computer that was used for word processing and administration. We had no internet, no mobile phones and the firm, one of the biggest in the world, did not have a website.

Certainly technology is one of the key factors that has enabled businesses to extend their reach and to grow in size globally, but there are also many other factors at play. For example, worldwide competition has meant that attention must be paid not only to the product being supplied but also to issues concerning service, quality, delivery and price. A breakdown in traditional socioeconomic barriers has meant that client purchasing loyalties are no longer based on local and historic relationships but on the best 'deal'. People will shop around, even for legal representatives, and issues relating to brand and differentiation in the marketplace are crucial to the ongoing success of any commercial business.

I left law in the early 1990s to do a masters in organizational psychology and now find that, like my fellow colleagues in the law, there is little need for me to travel daily to any office other than the client's, little need for a large room full of books, pens and paper, absolutely no need for a Dictaphone and even less need for a fax. I find that I can operate very successfully with my laptop, my mobile phone and a short blog or website. This way, I can be easily and instantly connected with any existing or potential clients, with colleagues, suppliers, collaborators and, of course, with my family and friends, albeit being physically apart from any one of them. I find that I can be both part of as well as separate from them. Indeed the more that I explore this topic of complexity, the more that it seems to me to incorporate both elements within it.

Interconnectedness

You, the reader, will of course have your own unique experience of how this changing world environment has impacted on you as an individual, your close relationships, the groups that you operate within, the businesses that you work for and your wider society and community. What I notice increasingly, as I work with clients, is that it is as if part of the problem of complexity in their lives is that all of these different levels are so inextricably interconnected that it can be difficult to see where they start, stop, begin or end. You may, for example, be reading this on your Kindle in an airport somewhere on your way to see a client in another country. At your side your laptop may be charging because you have some slides to finish off later for a presentation next week for your team. Meanwhile, you are also catching up on a flurry of e-mails, some of which you realize are increasingly urgent and, finally, you have also remembered that you must text your husband or wife to remind them about some extra-curricula school event for your child.

Perhaps you are a senior manager in a large supermarket chain and your flurry of e-mails is asking for an urgent response to a scandal that has just broken in the news. This concerns traces of horsemeat that were found in burgers on sale throughout the stores. It is transpiring that these must have been have been supplied by a distant subcontractor to one of your UK warehouses via various other contractors in different countries. What do you do? How do you respond? One can understandably become frozen and paralysed in the face of the enormity of the challenge, its complexity and its critical importance to the business. While mobile and paradoxically interconnected, you are also stuck here in an airport trying to assess this crisis on your own.

The emerging theme of interconnectedness is also curiously becoming more prevalent in other areas and domains of expertise. Take, for example, the new physics, where thinking has significantly shifted from the Newtonian notion of a simple, separate and fixed view of matter to one of randomness and chaos. Take economics, where the turmoil in the Western financial markets that came to a head in 2008 so clearly involved a number of key stakeholders, such that it was difficult to ascribe blame to the bankers alone. Instead, people were forced to ask what part was being played out in the whole economic system that enabled such chaos and devastation to occur. Where can you lay the blame? On the greedy borrowers? Or the greedy bankers? Or the boards and risk managers who failed to act competently? On the millions of institutional investors who allowed their boards to be rewarded with exorbitant bonuses? On the regulators who should have noticed what was going on? Or on the 'puritanical' Germans or the 'irresponsible' Greeks? Or maybe on you and me for not speaking up when we should have. This clearly demonstrates the interconnectedness of it all.

Socially, too, we see enormous increases in mobility and social networking where even revolutions can be orchestrated via social media sites. Tunisia in 2012 and Syria in 2013 are cases in point. Finally, there has recently been a subtle meeting of Eastern and Western philosophies evidenced perhaps by a rise in the West of mindfulness and other mediation practices that advocate a view of whole, community and oneness with life and the universe, and at the same time scandals and the demise in the role of separatist and individualist philosophies within institutions such as the Catholic church.

Purpose and intention

Arguably, complexity has been around ever since the beginning of time. Maybe we are just noticing it more now, especially since the advent of social media and other more transparent public forums. Perhaps the value of a good financial or other business crises is that it forces us to ask again about what matters. What has true value and meaning in life and our world? And thereby raise our levels of consciousness to begin to see things as they really are and might have always been. The question then is how do we successfully navigate our organizations through this? Part of the answer is by holding true to the core purpose and intention behind the organization. Why was it set up and in the service of what or who?

Certainly, there are numerous recent examples of organizations that, in the interests of continuous growth and expansion, lost sight of their core purpose and intention in the world, with devastating consequences for both themselves and many others. Let's look at some particular examples.

Case study Arthur Andersen (and Enron)

Mr Arthur E Andersen, founder of Arthur Andersen, is said to have cemented his reputation when he told a local railroad chief that there was not enough money in the whole of Chicago to persuade him to agree to enhance reported profits by using creative accounting. He lost the account – and the railroad firm went bankrupt soon after. Mr Andersen had a moral compass.

By the 1980s, the firm was adopting the Big Five auditors' new business model: grow the business by selling consultancy on the back of the audit relationship. Andersen did well. It embraced a '2x' model – bring in twice as much consultancy as audit revenue. Those who succeeded in doing this were rewarded, whereas those who did not perform faced sanctions. Fear of losing consultancy work must have pervaded the audit teams.

Through its work for Enron, Andersen earned $25 million in audit fees and $27 million in consultancy fees in the year 2000. Over the years, Andersen had been involved in creating and signing off 'creative' accounting techniques, such as aggressive revenue recognition and mark-to-market accounting, along with the creation of special purpose vehicles used for doubtful purposes. The firm was sufficiently concerned in 2001 for 14 partners, eight from the local office that handled Enron, to discuss whether they retained sufficient independence from Enron. Having observed that revenues could reach $100 million, they decided nonetheless to keep Enron's account. Andersen and Enron were both later to collapse. One suspects that Mr Andersen might not have reached the same conclusion as his 14 partners.

Case study Northern Rock

Northern Rock was a UK bank, formerly a mutual 'building society', which collapsed in September 2007. Building societies were mutual organizations, owned by their members, and relied mainly on funds deposited with them by members to make mortgage advances to other members. Ten years before the collapse, Northern Rock had demutualized and this conversion from mutual to commercial status increased the pressures to make profits and drive up the share price, with management holding share options. The consequences of this included fraudulent reporting and an aggressive business model.

The story then went as follows: On 12 September 2007 Northern Rock, having become the fifth largest UK mortgage lender, asks for liquidity support from the Bank of England. The next day, the BBC reported that the bank had asked for and received emergency financial support and, within hours, long queues began to form outside branch offices as depositors sought to withdraw their savings. £1 billion was withdrawn in one day, about 5 per cent of the bank's total deposits and around £2 billion was withdrawn within a couple of days. Northern Rock's phone lines were jammed and its website failed due to the volume of customers trying to log on and withdraw their funds from internet accounts. This was the first run on a UK bank since 1878. The share price fell by more than 50 per cent in a couple of days and the cost to the taxpayer of the bailout was ultimately £26 billion.

What went wrong? Well, many things went wrong but one of the most significant contributing factors was that the company had lost sight of its original purpose as a mutual; leadership had then pursued a high-risk and reckless business strategy and had failed to appreciate the importance of its stakeholders and of maintaining a bank's reputation for paying depositors on demand. This lack of appreciation of interconnectedness and context may also have been, at least in part, because neither the Chairman nor the CEO had been trained as bankers.

When organizations operate or expand mindlessly and recklessly in this way, it can become almost impossible for you, as a leader or manager, to work to purpose and be effective in your role. By contrast, when organizations are crystal clear about their core purpose and intention and work to align and include all stakeholders in that then you will find it much more manageable facing the varied and many challenges that will undoubtedly arise within your role. This is truer now than ever before as complexity and interconnectedness increasingly have their say.

Change

Whether you experience this uncertainty as a newish phenomenon in your working life or one that has always existed, the truth is that for most of us there is a real sense of things speeding up. Fifteen years ago I might have been asked about three or four times a year to work with a client on their 'change processes' whereas now change is an integral part of almost everything that a client needs. It is as if change has become a constant and we have all become acutely aware of its presence.

We can view this uncertainty solely through the lens of business or more broadly and beyond to society and the wider world in which we live. We can even go further, with a broader ecological lens, looking at climate change and patterns on the planet. In each domain we will find that same confusion arising; in each the future is becoming less and less clear. For most of us we are not sure which of the old road maps we can follow. We do not feel equipped to know what steps will enable us to get to where we need to be. John Scott, the Chief Risk Officer at Zurich Global Corporate, recently explained to me how the insurance industry tracks unusual and significant global phenomena (known because of their rarity as black swan events) in order to better predict risk in the future and therefore what steps to take in the present. These included events such as the recent floods in Australia, Superstorm Sandy in the United States and cybercrime in China. Superstorm Sandy alone cost the industry $86 billion and it is impossible to know what the recent financial crash cost both them and us in real money. Learning the right lessons from these events is therefore crucial for our success in the future.

Anxiety

It is as if crisis has become the new norm. The implications of this are that people are becoming increasingly anxious and uncertain within their roles in life and at work. This can lead to reduced effectiveness at work – a spiralling from anxiousness to poorer performance and back and forth and on and on.

Let me describe this reactive pattern of response by way of a model that I often use when working with clients. It is called the transition curve and is based on the work of Kübler-Ross (1969). Imagine a hypothetical situation of a manager changing roles. They have been promoted to a position of leading the Asian market for a large subsidiary, where before they had had a specialist function in Europe. The role presents them with a range of new options for behaviour, status and responsibility, as well as bringing enormous expectations from others. To succeed they will have to cope with this ambiguity and uncertainty. The transition curve looks at the psychological processes that the individual has to go through to really come to terms effectively with their new role and describes the journey in terms of seven distinct phases (see Figure 1.1).

Phase 1: Shock

Having been delighted with the promotion and feeling very competent, the first phase kicks in. It describes the reaction when the individual initially encounters something that they had not expected or anticipated in the role. Maybe people in the leadership team are not quite behaving as they had been expecting, leading to conflict, and projects are beginning to fall behind. Shock or surprise arises from the mismatch between the way in which the individual manager believes things might have been, and the way that they actually are. As can be seen from Figure 1.1, the individual's perceived

FIGURE 1.1 The transition curve (based on the work of Kübler-Ross)

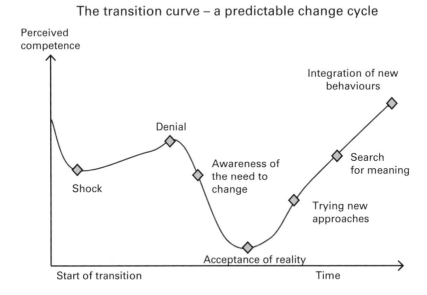

The transition curve – a predictable change cycle

competence or confidence (vertical axis) reduces in the face of the new change, which indicates their own sense of how 'good' they are in the new role; that is, their own sense of value in terms of ability to perform the new role effectively.

Confidence dips in this first phase as a result of the impact of experiencing the new set of circumstances or expectations that may not be as the manager expected them to be. The more unknown or unexpected these new circumstances, the deeper the dip, as there is a greater mismatch between expectations and reality. The individual will experience a larger negative impact on their sense of competence the more inaccurate their perception and the more unexpected the change. In extreme cases, this may lead to the individual manager feeling immobilized – that is, unable to make decisions or plans or giving the appearance of being unable to lead. Although this vertical axis reflects the individual's own sense of confidence and competence, it is an important indicator of performance as individuals' feelings of their effectiveness are strongly linked to their actual behaviour.

Phase 2: Denial

Following the shock stage comes a new period of denial, during which the individual makes his or her own conclusions about the new situation, in order to minimize the dissonance experienced in the first phase. This justification or reasoning of events prompts an increase in the individual's sense of competence – they gain a form of intellectual control over the situation. Let's take our hypothetical example above, of the promotion. A natural first reaction occurs: shock at the extent of the differences in this new role from the old one – an unexpected discovery in which the individual's perceptions did not match reality. In order to 'cope' with this change, the manager may try to deny the reality, for example, that the new role is not different after all; or he or she may try to explain it away, for example, by justifying that the markets are at fault, that competitor companies are also experiencing setbacks with their timelines and project delivery dates. Family and close colleagues may well collude in the denial. This is because for them too it is painful to have to consider changes, to be with the unknown versus the predictable and ultimately, of course, to face the possibility of the manager's failure and what this might mean for them. All of it can be difficult for them to bear too.

Moreover, if the manager believes that they were awarded the promotion based on track record rather than future potential, there is even less reason for them to change their behaviour or attitudes because 'what worked well in the past will work in the future'. This denial of the need to do anything differently can be a sticking point in the transition process and may well prevent the individual from ever moving on.

I have worked with many executives, helping them to get beyond this point, and whether this stage becomes for them a hill, as Figure 1.1 depicts, or more of a plateau, the only way to move forward from here is through individual choice. I cannot do the work for them and persuasion, encouragement or threat from within their organization may provoke only compliant behaviour. What is required here is a real awareness of the need for change at a personal level. Once this occurs, and frequently with it an awareness of the individual's strengths and weaknesses, the individual is able to accept others' views of himself or herself and the need to make the adjustment to achieve his or her potential. Individuals who are reluctant to make this change will be 'stuck' at this point in the transition; they are unable to accept a different view of themselves and of the need for the change to happen.

Phase 3: Awareness

While the previous phase corresponds with a perceived *increase* in competence, while the individual ignores the reality of the situation, the third phase brings with it a greater awareness of his or her *real* level of competence in relation to the required level. This is a vital stage of enquiry about the old role and the new one, about what has worked and what is not working. Ultimately, it is about what has to be let go of from the past in order to dive deeper into the new role. It is a critical stage as the individual becomes emotionally engaged in the situation and is frequently marked by feelings of fear, frustration, anger, rage, guilt and confusion. The old ways are not working. Areas that have now been defined as 'deficient' require attention and the individual may or may not know exactly how to do this, how to increase their level of skill or change their attitude.

Phase 4: Acceptance

The downward move in competence and confidence stops when the individual truly recognizes and accepts the reality of the new situation. They can see more clearly the cultural nuances that maybe before they were blind to; they can see where the conflict and intolerance have arisen and why; and they understand that this lack of alignment within the leadership team is creating the deadline delays. This is the lowest point on the figure. It requires a complete letting go of attitudes and behaviours which have before been comfortable and appropriate but are no longer effective for the new situation. Feelings of anxiety will occur as a result of not knowing what to put in place of those old behaviours and attitudes. The manager can be at a loss as to what to do next.

Phase 5: Trying new approaches

The manager then identifies and tries out new ways of working with the leadership team, testing them out together. Some of these new behaviours may be effective and achieve the desired outcome, some may need to be practiced or 'polished' and others will fail. Hence it may not be a simple progression from left to right as failure at trying out a new skill may push the individual back along the curve while the individual questions its relevance or searches for alternative behaviours.

This is a difficult time of 'trying on things for size' and seeing whether they fit. It can be time-consuming and potentially costly in its result. However, when working with organizations, I always have to especially encourage leaders and managers to allow for mistakes at this time. This is because companies that allow individuals to make mistakes, and not suffer recrimination for failure, create the most supportive types of environment for this part of the transition and ultimately for real and lasting change to occur.

Phase 6: Search for meaning

Letting go of what was needed in order to move effectively into their new role, and learning from their successes and failures, helps the individual to begin to see meaning in the new situation. Rather than just trying new behaviours on for size, this stage brings with it a deeper understanding of context; of why certain behaviours are effective and why others or indeed the same behaviours, but on a different occasion, may be ineffective. Ultimately, it will bring with it an understanding of why this experience may have been a useful learning experience for the individual. They arrive at this stage of the curve a more enlightened individual, made more competent by the journey that they have been on, and more able to go through a similar process again in the future.

Interestingly, the transition curve was first developed by Kübler-Ross when she was working with the dying in a hospice. You can imagine that this phase had very deep and great significance for her patients. These people had potentially been able to move through the curve experiencing anger, maybe as well as hurt, grief and loss, before being able to let go of what was no longer really needed in their life at this time. They will then have transitioned into a different way of being; perhaps being able to forgive or repair certain relationships that needed healing and ultimately making much more sense of the experience of their whole life as well as their death.

Phase 7: Integration

The final stage is characterized by the individual taking ownership of their recently acquired behaviours, thereby increasing their sense of confidence and competence to a higher level than before. Their new ways of doing things become part of their everyday activities and integrated into the individual's worldview and natural reaction. There is little or no dissonance between the expectations of situations and the individual's perceived own ability to perform.

Significant transition takes time and the cycle described above can take 12 to 18 months depending on the context. However, having an understanding of the process can greatly help along the journey. Additionally, previous experience of change and going through this cycle meaningfully can help to develop one's muscle and capacity for change and adaptation in the future.

Human nature

The model can also be applied at an organizational level, helping all those involved with change to make sense of their feelings and reactions during the period of transition. What I find is that when exploring it with clients, no matter how technically or analytically disposed they might be, once I begin to open up with them the notion of the feelings that might arise during phases three and four, there is nearly always an enormous sigh of relief in the room, as if somehow or other the 'cat is out of the bag'. Guess what? They are human with unconscious reactive and messy responses to work, each other and life. An equally revealing and relieving revelation is that so is everyone else in the room and indeed in the organization.

The model is, therefore, a useful way of seeing your inner world of subjective experience, feelings and emotional responses to situations at work. It is particularly useful for enabling a dialogue about more private, and maybe what might be seen initially as negative, feelings such as anger, fear, envy, shame and guilt. However, it is also useful for exploring more positive emotions and what might give us value, meaning and joy.

I have always wondered why this revelation should be the preserve only of a change process when we are also human, and therefore anxious, emotional and reactive, in the face of the normal day-to-day job on a Monday morning. Of course, the difference is that there is the heightened anxiety and excitement that comes with change which triggers more acute and extreme feelings. However, if crisis and change have become the new organizational norm, then the reality is that many of us will find that we are actually going through this cycle on a continuous basis. It follows that developing the insight and skill to better understand and navigate your way through the seven stages outlined above will not only be helpful, but perhaps essential, in enabling you to perform your day-to-day role as a leader and manager within your organization.

The challenge of letting go

The fact is that change is a constant. The moment is always about to change. We move from birth to childhood, on to school, friends and then work. Maybe later we become parents and then ultimately we face the inevitability of death. We are each of us in a constant cycle of change, not knowing what might happen next. In our attempt to create an illusion of safety we hang on to old patterns and ways of behaving that are based on our experience of the past and that in many ways no longer work for us or our organizations going forward. We build this fantasy that if somehow we were clever enough or dedicated enough we would be able to control events and we are deeply resistant to letting go of our confidence in that illusion for fear of our shame in not knowing what might replace it.

So if, in your role, complexity has become a given and change a constant your anxiety levels may understandably be heightened in the face of this uncertainty and not knowing. It will help you greatly to navigate your way through this uncertain landscape if you can:

- make the conscious decision to align with organizational purpose and intention;
- be willing to embrace and explore any resulting behavioural changes that will be required in the knowledge that this will mean your letting go of old ways of seeing and relating; and
- be willing to be with the fact that this is rarely a comfortable or easy process because it means accepting that you are not perfect or in control.

Let me say, however, that as a discipline and a cultivated way of being, it will be worth your while because this will give you access to tremendous energy, power and creativity and ultimately enable you to more easily realize success.

The models and techniques described in Part 2 of this book are an invitation for you to explore your own patterns of response when working in role and see more clearly where tweaks or adjustments may be required. They are also an opportunity for you to explore how you relate to others and how you operate within working groups. This is the first of my two-pronged approach to the enlightened organization, the personal and interpersonal, and is designed to help you build better relationship capability. The techniques will enable you to more skilfully operate within these uncertain business times and to become more influential in helping your fellow colleagues, stakeholders and organization to make a real difference in the world.

Before we get there, however, in Chapter 2 we will look at the way in which complexity and change is catching up on organizational structures and ways of doing business. Then later, in Chapter 3, at the implications of this in terms of managing and leading your part of the business. In Part 3, we will move on to the second part of the two-pronged approach to look at system and context. This is so that you can develop a real understanding of your operating environment and the unique challenges and opportunities that it presents.

KEY POINTS

1 Complexity and interconnectedness are a given in the global organizational landscape that is emerging.

2 Change is now a constant and the new norm.

3 People experience a heightened sense of anxiety in the face of increasing levels of uncertainty and not knowing.

4 It will help you greatly as a leader or manager within your organization to understand where you are at any point in time on the transition curve.

5 In particular, alignment with organizational purpose, making a conscious decision and commitment to work with change, accepting your own limitations and cultivating a spirit of inquiry about what adjustments the context and purpose might, at any

time, require will help you to more skilfully operate within this changing paradigm.

6 Organizations don't change or do business or, as I pointed out in the Introduction, read books. But you do all three. You are, therefore, critical to the success of your business and a key player in enabling it to manifest the purpose for which it was created in the world.

A new reality for organizations

02

Managing risk and reputation

> *Appearance is something absolute, but reality is not that way – everything is interdependent, not absolute.* **DALAI LAMA**

Complexity is catching up on companies and their way of doing business just as much as it is on individuals, so that companies too are experiencing the effects of greater interconnectedness and the speed of change. This is forcing new structures for the way that they organize themselves in relation to the world and even larger questions about their purpose and role in the wider scheme of things. These pressures are, in my view, calling them to take a more enlightened approach and to the heart of what really matters in business, whether some of them want to travel in that direction or not.

What has heart, value and meaning is no less relevant for the whole organization than it is for its individual members and leads me to challenge the assumption that businesses exist solely to make money. While making money may be a result of the business, and is essential to the continued functioning of the business, it is not its purpose. An intake of oxygen, while essential for our living, is not the purpose of our lives. Perhaps the time has come when we could, instead, think about the role of business in broader terms: in terms of improving society by creating organizations that people want to work for, that people want to do business with, and that people want to invest in for the longer term. In effect, to aspire to make this world a better place by reaching its fullest potential through the limitless possibilities of its people.

When I first started consulting as an organizational psychologist, I had the good fortune to attend a lecture given by Charles Handy at the Royal Society for the encouragement of Arts, Manufactures and Commerce (1995). He was delivering a paper entitled 'What is a company for?', which challenged the continued focus on short-term share price as a symbol of success. It brought to light the concept of businesses being viewed as wealth-creating communities with responsibility for environmental and social sustainability. Ironically, Handy's lecture was delivered in the midst of the Enron and WorldCom scandals and his philosophy was then ignored in the finance world. Over the subsequent 10 years, a large number of lending institutions continuously sought immediate short-term profit and success with an almost complete disregard for the future and the world around them; this by taking advantage of naïve customers which caused a ripple effect that has been devastating in many parts of the Western world.

The system

New organizational structures

Old reality

In Figure 2.1, I have outlined the changing typography of the commercial operating environment. In the old reality organizations were hierarchical, bureaucratic and relatively static and fixed in their nature. With this model, organizations are seen as separate from their environment; their internal departments separate from each other and individual employees as assets or commodities performing their daily tasks. The workforce and client base are largely homogenous, loyal and almost completely stable, often staying with the company for life. The methodologies applied to perform the work are tried and tested from the past. Provided all of the above is managed and kept in check, then the product remains the same and the business can be almost guaranteed a stable share price and consistent market share and growth.

Current reality

At this moment in time organizations are, in my view, mostly operating from the current reality (see Figure 2.1) where the structure is

FIGURE 2.1 New organizational structures

New Organizational Structures		
Old Reality	**Current Reality**	**New Reality**
Bureaucracy	Flat hierarchy	Networks
Assets	Core competency	Visions/values
Market share	Share of wallet	Share of heart
Operator	Resource	Talent
Employment	Competencies	Relationship
Charisma	Competencies	Trust-based relationship
Homogeneity	Diversity	Inclusion

that of a matrix or flat hierarchy. The matrix is less fixed and static in its form than the old bureaucratic paradigm and people will have two or more formal locations on the organizational chart. Within this model, organizations are seen as separate as well as part of their external environment; internal departments and teams increasingly work with others and individual employees are engaged as competent and often specialized resources required for the now ever-changing nature of the evolving task.

There is a rise in the number of critical stakeholders to the business including employees, clients, collaborators, suppliers, regulators, the press and the wider community. These are no longer loyal stable relationships 'for life'. Instead relationships are temporary, remote, mobile and completely diverse. The methodologies applied to perform the work are re-evaluated and revised as a function of what arises within the changing business landscape and the business cannot be managed in the traditional sense of implementing a known strategy; it must instead be led. The product cannot stay the same if the business is to compete and there is absolutely no guarantee of a stable share price or increased market share and growth.

New reality

But in truth even this model is not going to work for the future. Something completely different will be required, a much looser framework with semi-permeable boundaries between the organization and its environment and between the multiple stakeholders. Something where, as an organic and evolving network of relationships, the organization interacts with and learns from its context, from its interconnectedness and from what is emerging as its future. The shape of this is outlined in my new reality (see Figure 2.1).

Stakeholder relationships give shape to the semi-permeable boundary of the system, each stakeholder being themselves invested in the success of the operation. These relationships are now often shared with other businesses and can sometimes last for only as long as they are needed for the task. Talented staff are vital, as there are few established methodologies that can be applied, and often judgement and professional wisdom followed by immediate action is required. Trust and inclusion have come to replace competency and diversity in order to enable the ongoing discernment of purpose and the self-authorization of all. Management and the more traditional forms of leadership will no longer enable a fixed strategy to be created. Instead the focus will be moved down and throughout the organization to all of its people so that they, as they interconnect with the outside, wider global context, can each be continuously enquiring as to what the world requires from this organization at this point in time and for the future. The product or service to be supplied will no longer always be known in advance but instead emerge and the longer-term and systemic impact of the business will become as important and relevant a measure of success as short-term share price, market share and growth.

Changing psychological contract

This calls for a new psychological contract between the organization and its employees. Traditionally, within the old model, a relative degree of security, in terms of a fair salary and prospects for the future, would have been sufficient to ensure loyalty and high performance on the part of individual employees, thereby ensuring that both parties were happy to stay together. Now, however, some other form of glue or centripetal force will be required. Like atomic particles, the diverse elements of this new organic network will instead have to have a kind of magnetic form of cohesion similar to the laws of attraction in science. That can only be created by a strong sense of shared purpose, common values and a real understanding of what has heart and meaning for all the varied stakeholders in the business.

The enlightened organization realizes that within the future paradigm its people are critical to the development of its key networks: to the winning of hearts and minds; to the selling of brand and maintaining of reputation; to the co-creation of trust and inclusion and to the avoidance of risk – which we will look at later in this chapter. That they, and only they, can, in this complex, interconnected and changing context enable the strategic direction of the business to emerge and only they can realize its fulfilment. So the alignment and fit between the person and the role, the purpose of the organization and its individuals, and the genuine passion of both in terms of what has heart, value and meaning are all areas that will become ever more critical for the future.

Fresh thinking

Operating in this future way will require a new way of thinking about business as well as asking questions about its role and purpose in society. Old assumptions will undoubtedly be challenged, such as that the purpose of any business is solely to make money. Instead we might, in time, come to see that organizations, being shaped by their context, are an integral part of all of co-creation. We might come to see:

- Organizations appreciating that they are not simply the sum of their outputs and perhaps have a broader purpose, which is to enable their context and the people operating within it to fulfil their potential in the world.

- Organizations becoming more aware of the deeper intentions behind their business. As Handy asks 'What is this company for?' The answer will be unique and potentially limitless and often paradoxically more easily answered by listening to the context and what might be required of it in the world.

- Barriers between competing elements within the business can be destroyed and replaced with a sense of common work to be done.

- Businesses seeing themselves as intricately connected to the world around them and learning to follow a simple rule whereby they treat all stakeholders (including, for example, customers, suppliers, competitors, governments and distributors) that they interact with as part of themselves, and seeking the best for all involved parties, and as a result themselves benefitting the most.

- A growing realization that the real purpose of the organization is only achieved over time and that a longer-term perspective will create success in both the longer, as well as the shorter, term.

The context

We have choices, both as individuals and as organizations, about the way in which we choose to live and operate. We can proceed, as we might have done before, bobbing along the surface of events as they arise, and doing our best that way. Or we can choose to become more fully conscious and awake, taking more responsibility for the emergence and shape of our collective future.

I suggest that the enormous speed of change is forcing us to have to reconsider that choice. What are the risks if we don't? What are the very real consequences if we choose not to adapt in the ways that I spoke about earlier?

Roads to ruin and managing reputation

Living life and being in business will always carry risks but whereas before a weak business model or faulty product might have cost the business money, its effect was unlikely to put the company totally out of business. Today, by contrast, companies are growing in size and diversifying. Customers' loyalties are changing, giving rise to a very real need for brand differentiation. And the advent of social media is such that the speed with which news, good and bad, can travel in our world, means that one bad move can simply bring a company down. It follows that the management of business reputation is becoming of critical importance.

Let me highlight some examples of this point from a piece of research by Cass Business School for Airmic, *Roads to Ruin: A study of major risk events: Their origins, impact and implications* (2011) (the Roads to Ruin research, reproduced here with the kind permission of Airmic). This research investigates the origins and impact of over 20 major corporate crises of the previous decade and identifies the key lessons associated with the failure to prevent each crisis and thereafter manage the consequences.

Substantial, well-known organizations were included in the study, such as Arthur Andersen, Enron and Northern Rock, which we looked at earlier in Chapter 1. Others included were Coca-Cola, Firestone, Shell, BP, Airbus, Société Générale, Cadbury Schweppes, AIG, Independent Insurance, Railtrack, the UK Passport Agency and also some smaller firms.

Several of these organizations simply did not survive and many suffered very costly consequences, for both their immediate as well as their most distant stakeholders. This was the case with Northern Rock, where it was the UK taxpayer who had to ultimately bail the bank out at a cost of £26 billion. Many senior leaders, such as Ken Lay, the chairman at Enron, were convicted for the part they played in their company's demise and went to prison. Other senior leaders, while they may have escaped this time, will undoubtedly have learnt some severe lessons and understand more about the catastrophic consequences that can ensue when reputation and brand are damaged. They are unlikely to get away with such reckless behaviour again if holding similar positions in the future.

An interesting point to note about the Roads to Ruin research was that everything looked at was already freely available in the public domain. The researchers did not interview company employees or, otherwise, do any further investigations – the point being that business reputation is about how one is perceived in the world not necessarily what one has actually done. It is also becoming increasingly difficult to undo the enormous damage done to reputation once anything adverse, whether in fact it is actually true or not, appears in the public domain.

Let me share some specific examples from the study, which highlight the themes that I have referred to in the two-pronged approach and Chapter 1. In particular:

- the implications of complexity and global interconnectedness;
- the importance of working to purpose;

- the challenge of letting go and working with change;
- the need to focus on the longer term; and finally
- how vital it is to have a real understanding and appreciation of the system and the context within which the business is operating.

Case study: Northern Rock

I outlined the story of Northern Rock in Chapter 1. To recap, the bank had demutualized and this conversion from mutual to commercial status increased the pressures to make profits and drive up the share price, with management holding share options. The consequences of this included fraudulent reporting and an aggressive business model. The bank was ultimately bailed out by UK taxpayers at a cost of £26 billion.

What went wrong? Well, as outlined before, many things but to highlight a few: the company had lost sight of its original purpose as a mutual; leadership in pursuing a high-risk and reckless business strategy had failed to appreciate the importance of its stakeholders and of maintaining a bank's reputation for paying depositors on demand. This lack of appreciation of interconnectedness and context may have been, at least in part, because neither the Chairman nor the CEO had been trained as bankers. And arguably, the run could have been stopped on the evening of the announcement that the Bank of England was acting as lender of last resort to the bank. But neither the CEO nor the Chairman took the only step that might possibly have succeeded: namely getting the message over to depositors that their money was now safe.

Maclaren

In this case, reported child injuries (finger amputations) in the United States involving pushchairs led to a major product recall. Maclaren, a UK company owned by a US investor with its manufacturing operations based in China, was not seen as applying a similar standard of post-event action in Europe by contrast to the United States. The result was damage to the brand, with the press and social media sites playing a large role in communicating complaints from stakeholders. The company realized that their response needed to be looked at from the outside context and from the different vantage points of all of its critical stakeholders. Only then could it see that it needed to apply a similar level of post-event action in Europe. Prior to this the European press and social media sites had been great advocates for the company and so the company had not anticipated or been prepared for this changed position.

Arthur Andersen

I pointed out in Chapter 1 that one of the reasons for the demise of Arthur Andersen was that part of its operations in the United States had become involved in creating and signing off 'creative' accounting techniques, such as aggressive revenue recognition and mark-to-market accounting for a large client in the United States, Enron.

However, it was largely the stories about shredding documents, Andersen's top management refusing to testify at congressional hearings and the fact that they received a felony conviction, that destroyed Andersen's reputation and the viability of its international practices outside the United States. Although the District Court felony conviction was subsequently overturned, on appeal to the Supreme Court, it was then too late to resurrect and rebuild the worldwide brand.

Key underlying risks

The Roads to Ruin research analysed these major corporate crises and identified seven key underlying risks that were at cause:

- inadequate leadership on ethos and culture;
- inappropriate incentives, both implicit and explicit;

- organizational complexity and change;
- defective internal communication and information flow;
- inadequate skills at board and the most senior levels of management;
- blindness to inherent risks, such as to the business model or reputation; and
- 'glass ceiling' effects that prevent managers from addressing risks emanating from top echelons.

Let's see, by way of example, and of course with the benefit of hindsight, how some of these scenarios might have played out differently if some of these risks had been identified and addressed.

Inadequate leadership on ethos and culture

Arthur Andersen is again a case in point. What if the partners had retained the moral compass of its founder and decided to cease working for Enron? Might both companies still be in business?

Another example is Cadbury. Here was a company with a Quaker-inspired moral history. During Todd Spitzer's period as CEO, Cadbury had a central catchphrase to describe its approach – 'Performance Driven, Values Led'. This highlighted a dilemma at the heart of Cadbury's new strategy: was performance to be the priority? Or values? Or were they to be equal? In 2006, Cadbury's recalled some of their products because of a very minute possibility of their being contaminated by salmonella. They delayed the product recall by five months because of a recent company policy that had increased the tolerance level of salmonella from zero to finite but low, on the (incorrect) assumption that a very low level of salmonella was safe. They were later prosecuted for selling unsafe products and failing to report the problem immediately. The court prosecutor argued that the tolerance increase was to reduce costs. What if Cadbury had prioritised values over performance?

Inappropriate incentives, both implicit and explicit

Equally BP, a company that suffered serious reputational damage when the Deepwater Horizon disaster occurred in 2010, had a similar contradiction with its twin focus on safety and financial performance. What was to prevail? Safety or performance? At BP the conflict was implicitly resolved – in favour of financial performance – by the executive incentive scheme. This allocated 70 per cent of bonus to performance and 15 per cent to safety. But what if the bonus scheme had been 70 per cent safety and 15 per cent performance? Would the accident have occurred?

Another one of the financial institutions that suffered severe damage in the 2008 'crash' was AIG, where people were known to be 'blown up' if they did not meet their numbers. This led to records being altered to boost results during the period 2000 to 2005. Meanwhile, in one of its subsidiary companies AIGFP, 50 per cent of the large bonuses, set at the top, were dependent on short-term performance and were immediately available – the 'Traders Option'. This undoubtedly skewed performance towards short-term bonuses based on profits that were only made possible by 'free-riding' on the parent company's 'assumed' substantial capital and its AAA credit rating. In 2008, AIG's losses were $99 million. It was ultimately rescued by the US Federal Reserve in an operation that required funds of $182 billion to be made available. Five people were jailed for conspiracy and fraud. What if the incentives had instead been designed to reward performance over the longer term? There would then have been no pressure to hide losses and the business could have evolved naturally in line with the market.

Organizational complexity and change

The EADS Airbus A380 case in 2006 involved immense complexity at the levels of aircraft design, IT, technology, procurement, manufacture and assembly. Additional complexity was caused by political demands that work be shared 'fairly' between the different operations in the United Kingdom, France, Germany and Spain (which did not share technology platforms). Furthermore there was an insistence that the management structure should preserve a delicate Franco–German balance, with two CEOs, one from each country. This multi-dimensional complexity lay at the root of the debacle in which it was discovered that the wiring in the different aircraft sections, designed and made in different countries, would not mate properly when the assemblies were brought together at Toulouse, leading to very costly production delays.

How might things have worked out if the board had instead foreseen some of the risks involved in such a complex operation, so that the complexity itself was appreciated as carrying significant risk? Might they, in anticipating some of the potential problems, have been able to surface the important conversations in time to recover the situation?

What if people had been encouraged to speak up? Instead, middle managers kept the problem of non-matching aircraft sections from senior managers for six months. The politically sensitive nature of the project was discovered to have silenced criticism.

Defective internal communication

We saw that because of political sensitivity middle managers at Airbus kept the problem of non-matching aircraft sections from senior managers for six months.

In the case of Independent Insurance, Enron and AIG there was found to be poor internal communication about problems because of the hectoring and bullying behaviours of leadership. This blocked internal routes to non-executive board members who were then unaware of what was going wrong. Enron's chairman, Ken Lay, received a letter from a 'whistle-blower' who feared 'a wave of accounting scandals'. When Lay eventually met the writer, the inquiry he instigated was ineffectual. He asked the company's lawyers to investigate. They asked Arthur Andersen. The company lawyers said that it was 'OK if Andersen said it was OK'. Perhaps Lay preferred not to receive bad news but what if, instead, the whistle-blower had been really listened to and their concerns followed through on? Might the company have survived?

Inadequate skills at board and the most senior levels of management

Neither the CEO nor the Chairman at Northern Rock had had any systematic training in banking. Enron's non-executive board members were selected for their connections rather than for their skills and, in the lead-up to the Texas City explosion in 2005, the BP director who had board responsibility for all operations at BP's refineries, including safety, had no refining experience prior to his appointment. What if, instead, the Chairman of Northern Rock had for example been qualified to understand and appreciate its client depositors? What if he had spoken out publicly and reassured them at that critical moment when the Bank of England had stepped in? Arguably that may have stopped the run on the bank and its subsequent bailout.

Blindness to inherent risks, such as to the business model or reputation

What if the boards of AIG and Independent Insurance had questioned how their companies were producing exceptionally – and consistently – good results? Neither Independent Insurance's auditor, nor its actuary, nor its regulator seems to have heeded the prevailing market view that Independent's results were just 'too good to be true'.

'Glass ceiling' effects that prevent managers from addressing risks emanating from top echelons

Examples of 'glass ceiling' effects included internal controls such as internal audit and risk management at Independent Insurance and Enron not being strong enough to prevent fraud on the part of executives. But there were also many other examples, including the rogue trader Jérôme Kerviel at Société Générale who cost the bank nearly €5 billion despite warnings from the compliance team to his superiors.

Building resilience

The seven underlying risks highlighted here are potentially inherent in any organization. If they are unrecognized and unmanaged they can pose a lethal threat to the future of even the largest and most successful of businesses. It is, as we will see in the next chapter, increasingly a crucial part of the role of leadership and management of any organization to seek out, identify and address these risks going forward.

The Roads to Ruin research highlights the danger that these risks will remain unmanaged unless organizations recognize the need to deal with them. Unless they engage enlightened leaders and managers with enhanced vision and competencies in terms of understanding the complex, interconnected and changing context within which their business operates and the essential need for everyone's alignment with purpose. In reinforcing the importance of system and context and its interrelationship with the personal, the research says:

> The seven overreaching risk areas described earlier are fundamental to ethos, safety, reputation and longevity of organizations and to its ability to use its information effectively. However, they seem to be rarely discussed either by firms or in the literature on risk analysis. Many are virtually taboo internally because they touch on behaviour, decisions, performance and perceptions of senior echelons. Without listening to outsides, boards can only see themselves as in a mirror. They are vulnerable to 'group think'. They cannot see themselves as others do. They face the risk of self-deception.

It is for these reasons that system and context are at the heart of my two-pronged approach, alongside the personal and interpersonal. For, as can be seen from the above case studies, if, for example, purpose is unclear and maybe the organization has grown in complexity; or communication is poor; or incentives are mismatched to purpose; then no amount of self-actualization on the part of some key individuals, be they leaders or managers, will be sufficient to prevent a possible demise of the company. Attention is always needed on both sides of the model, both sides of the tuning fork: at the individual in terms of the personal and the interpersonal and at the organizational in terms of system and context, embracing and connecting the parts as well as the whole.

To conclude, businesses need to think seriously about what has heart, value and meaning for them and in that respect what is their real purpose and brand. They then need to safeguard the sanctity of this brand and their reputation. If they really want to be successful or, at the very least resilient, they will have to adopt a strategic and integrated policy that recognizes and deals with the risks outlined above and to incentivize all employees to stick rigidly to it.

The enlightened organization

Organizations that meaningfully embrace some or all of the above will, I suggest, be way ahead of the game in terms of rising to the challenges of their future. They will be far better equipped to work with the inevitability of complexity, interconnectedness and change, and be able to raise the bar globally in terms of business consciousness and success.

However, as mentioned in Chapter 1, organizations cannot read this book. But you can, as a manager and leader and on behalf of your organization, the implications of which we are going to look at in Chapter 3.

KEY POINTS

1 Complexity and change is affecting the way in which organizations are able to do business in the world and also challenging them in relation to their purpose and role within the wider scheme of things.

2 New organizational structures are emerging that reflect the changing typography of the business landscape and require a different type of psychological contract with employees; one which is more subtly based on alignment and realignment around shared purpose and intention.

3 Fresh thinking would enable organizations to see how they are fundamentally shaped by their context and an integral part of all of co-creation.

4 Brand and reputation have assumed a level of critical importance.

5 A deep appreciation of risk and reputation and being able to then build organizational resilience is now part and parcel of your day job as a leader and manager. This forms the basis of the two-pronged approach, in terms of addressing and fine tuning the personal and interpersonal alongside system and context.

Leaders and managers taking up their role
New skills and competencies required

03

> *Pathmaker, there is no path;*
> *You make the path by walking,*
> *By walking you make the path.*

ANTONIO MACHADO, AS QUOTED BY DAVID WHYTE

Interconnectedness is a given, change a constant and it is as if things are really speeding up – all of which is forcing new structures on the way in which we organize ourselves in business and raising bigger questions about purpose, values and what ultimately has heart and meaning for ourselves as well as our organizations and varied stakeholders.

What is certain, however, is that the role of leadership and management is changing considerably and that something altogether very different is emerging within the new reality outlined in Figure 2.1 (see page 25). Something that hangs more on the ability to see clearly the context within which the business operates as well as the ability to work more deeply with interconnectedness.

FIGURE 3.1 CEO's and SEO's traditional competency profile

Strengths	Shadow Side
• Confidence	• Opinionated, arrogant
• Energy/enthusiasm	• Impulsive, moody
• A doer	• Reckless, impulsive
• Global vision	• Misses the immediate
• A thinker	• Indecisive, lacks heart
• Has integrity	• Rigid, critical, zealot
• Independence	• Self-absorbed
• Charismatic	• Spin, ignores errors

Old competencies

The issue that some of the organizations in the Roads to Ruin research, referred to in Chapter 2, faced was that they were solving next-generation problems with leaders and managers who grew up in the old paradigm while operating in the current existing reality (see Figure 2.1 on page 25).

These leaders and managers had traditionally been hired, developed and rewarded for their individual competency and skill as 'solo performers'. They have been accepted without regard to their weaker shadow side and, in particular, their level of competency in terms of collaborating with others and leading through these increasingly networked times. They were, therefore, ill-equipped to create the future through integrating common values, developing trust and connecting heart and brand. Figure 3.1 offers a snapshot of what would have been and might still, in many instances, be a fairly typical leadership and management profile.

The Roads to Ruin researchers even went as far as to suggest that further investigation be carried out as to whether the weaknesses inherent within a traditional competency profile, as outlined in Figure 3.1, might be linked to a propensity for reputational crisis. They remarked:

A number of these risk areas we have identified concern the so-called 'soft' skills (staff, style and shared values) as opposed to the so-called 'hard' skills (technical know-how, strategy, structure and systems).

A valuable question for further investigation in this area is whether there is a causal link between weaknesses in leaders and board composition with respect to the so-called 'soft' skills and the propensity to suffer major reputational crises. (Cass Business School/Airmic, 2011)

New skills required

The significant themes emerging for organizations today are about context, purpose and interconnectedness. They can only ever succeed in this new operating environment to the extent that they are led and managed accordingly. It follows that leaders and managers for the future need to be able to:

- see more clearly the overall context within which they are operating;
- source and nurture the core purpose of their business;
- contain the anxiety of complexity and change for others;
- establish a culture of openness, dialogue and responsible behaviour;
- build collaborative relationships both within and beyond their industry sector because resilience can no longer be defined at the level of any individual business;
- engage hearts and minds enabling strategies and the future to emerge;
- enable quality strategic conversations throughout every level of the business including the boardroom; and
- promote disagreement as an asset as well as being able to ask better and better questions. (Tomorrow's Good Governance Forum, 2012)

The purpose of this book is to give you these skills. You may see all of this in terms of possibilities, the glass being half full, or through fear and resistance in terms of seeing the glass as half empty. However, the fact of the matter is that we all need to embrace these broad themes if we, and our organizations, are to survive economically and compete. The challenge for the organization, as we will see in Parts 3 and 4, will be how best to attract, develop, reward and retain people with these skills. The challenge for you as an individual is to develop the new competencies required by attending to Part 2 of this book. Hence my two-pronged approach to the enlightened organization.

Before moving on, however, I want first to look at some of the broad themes that are outlined above and what these might mean in terms of the new skills required for the role. The practical exercises that will help you to develop these skills are then contained in Part 2.

Embodying and defending purpose

We saw in Chapter 2, how a strong sense of shared purpose, common values and a real understanding of what has heart and meaning for the varied stakeholders to the business will be essential in the new reality. These are required in order to form the glue or centripetal force around which varied stakeholders, like atomic particles, can coalesce and then do the work that is required of them. It follows that one of the critical roles of leadership will be to define, embody and defend purpose and, as mentioned above, many of the exercises in Part 2 will help you with that.

In that sense it can be helpful to think in terms of leadership and followership and how we each can choose to take up either role depending on what is required by the context. In the new reality, the focus has largely moved down throughout the whole organization, to all its people as they busily interact with the outside world. They too need to be continuously enquiring as to what is required of them and the organization in terms of embodying and defending purpose. Obviously there will some people in the organization, such as the CEO, who by operating at a very strategic level may be said to be fulfilling the role of leadership more or less all of the time. But for the rest of us, there will be seasons for things, meaning that we will find ourselves increasingly moving in and out of the two separate roles.

Working with interconnectedness

One could write a whole book on this topic alone, but let me make a few important distinctions. First, being interconnected will be essential in order that the right business strategy can emerge and be realized. It will be this attunement with people, both within and outside of the organization, that will enable clarity and good judgement as well as the capacity to deliver.

Second, interconnectedness will also help determine whether leadership or management is, at any time, required. The distinction being that leadership is needed when the way ahead is uncertain: the task then being to defend purpose and discern the right steps to take; to decide on the most effective path. Once that work is done, management can take over working to implement the steps that have been decided upon. While there is a lot of turbulence and change in the market that requires leadership, there is always also an awful lot of normal day-to-day activities for which management is more appropriate.

Third, organizations will only see themselves as in a mirror if they do not engage meaningfully with their external context. The dangers of this are covered throughout the rest of the book, particularly in Parts 3 and 4.

Building relationship capability

An organizational structure that is built on networks, values, share of heart, trust and inclusion as, outlined in Figure 2.1 (see page 25), needs relationship capability as the air with which to breathe. The enlightened organization realizes that within the new reality this is critical to the development of key networks, to the winning of hearts and minds, to the selling of brand and maintaining of reputation, to the co-creation of trust and inclusion, and to the avoidance of the type of risks that we looked at in the last chapter.

In terms of a core competency, this means developing exceptional emotional intelligence ('EQ'). EQ is the ability to be aware of your different emotions and see the direct impact that they have on your performance, as we saw earlier in Chapter 1 with the transition curve. This involves a number of different steps and, as with everything else in life, the more consciously that you can practice these steps (which are outlined below), the more that the skill will become more readily available to you when you need it most.

As we saw in Chapter 1, we will often be anxious in the face of uncertainty, change and not knowing, and this anxiety can lead to reactive and defensive patterns of behaviour such as denial or resistance. This is unhelpful to us in our role and will ultimately impact greatly on our performance, those we lead or manage and ultimately the business. The exercise below is intended to strengthen your ability to work more consciously with your emotions, including anxiety, enabling you to become less reactive. Then instead when faced with a challenging situation of, for example, moving directly into denial or resistance you can, in noticing where you are headed, stop and begin to choose a more appropriate response. The exercise involves observing your state of being on a regular basis and with curiosity and non-judgement, so that you can develop the muscle of noticing what is actually going on for you at any point in time, right here, right now.

The more that you can do this for yourself, then the more easily you will be able to recognize emotional states and needs in others and therefore what they might need from you and your organization. Also, the more that you can treat your own experience in context seriously, the more you will find yourself connecting with others inside and outside of the organization in surprising ways; ways that would otherwise have been unavailable. This will then release the currently untapped resources of all. It is for this reason that developing a keen EQ can help you greatly in terms of building relationship capability and being more effective within the emerging new reality, which, as outlined before, is becoming increasingly relational.

EXERCISE 3.1 My now

- How are you feeling?

- Where is that feeling located in your body ie tight shoulders or fast heartbeat?

- What is it exactly? Can you give it a name or a label?

- Allow yourself to accept and let the feeling just be there as it is without trying to suppress or change it in any way.

- Ask yourself why you think this particular feeling is arising. Where do you think it might have come from?

- Enquire into what it is that the feeling might be telling you about what you need right now.

- With this new knowledge and insight see what choices might be available to you in terms of a response?

LIBRARY, UNIVERSITY OF CHESTER

Enabling change

One of the very real challenges that organizations, and therefore leaders and managers, face is the extent to which they are being presented with new unknowns. This is something that demands a response outside of their current toolkit and the gap between aspirations and operational capacity cannot be closed by the expertise and procedures currently in place. Take something very new like the internet or cloud computing, each of which require a whole new way of doing business. Dr Ron Heifetz (2009) talks about this in terms of adaptive challenges that require adaptive leadership.

We saw with the transition curve, in Chapter 1, that people can experience a significant personal journey when going through this type of change. The task of leadership is to help guide them through that process, to the new reality that is emerging and becoming distinct, albeit maybe only initially for the leader. That requires the ability to be able to move between high levels of abstract thinking to low levels of concrete action to discover where people need help; the establishment of a change process and the avoidance of premature closure or asking the tough questions.

Kegan and Lahey (2009) describe the type of thinking that is required for large adaptive change as the self-transforming mind. When taking on this role, leaders lead to learn; they hold contradictions; they problem-find and they act interdependently. All that to be better able to perform within the complex, interconnected and radically changing environment that I have described in Chapter 2.

Using conflict as a resource

I said above that one of the critical roles of leadership is to define, embody and defend purpose. That requires alignment and continuous realignment with key stakeholders, not all of whom will see eye to eye all of the time. It will, of course, be the very nature of their diversity and differences that adds value to the organization in terms of its depth and breath. It follows that to do alignment well, leaders and managers will have to be able to handle conflict. Indeed, they need increasingly in the new reality to learn to be able to use this as a valuable resource. Only then, as Dr Ron Heifetz points out, can they orchestrate the conflicts that arise and develop experiments 'to find out how to push the frontiers forward in an evolutionary way'.

To achieve this you will need to be able to listen to the music, the songs beneath the words and what these say about divided loyalties and interests that are perceived to be at stake and need protecting. You need to avoid the temptation of arrogance and ask yourself 'What if they are right?'

Letting go of knowing

It is worth reinforcing a point made earlier, in Chapter 1, that the challenge for you as an individual is also ultimately about being able to operate with uncertainty and not knowing. This is an uncomfortable place for most of us, but perhaps especially for those in senior positions where, more often than not, you expect and are expected to know the 'right' answers.

The need to know will force premature closure and stop people from asking the difficult questions. In an adaptive challenge, the leader cannot know what they are doing because it is, by its very nature, a new edge or frontier – an edge where everyone will be in over their heads. This is why thinking in terms of the role can be more helpful. That way, we question the notion that leadership means 'I know where we are going. Just follow me.' This old paradigm puts an enormous amount of pressure on leaders to fake it and provide quick technical fixes that tend to ignore the larger, more important ones. In the words of Ralph Stacey (2003), the challenge is:

> how to cope with not knowing... It is quite natural not to know and this does not have to incapacitate one. It is possible to carry on working together even in the condition of not knowing. Self-organising conversational processes operating in the state of not knowing producing emergent meaning, often of a new and creative kind.

Leaders and managers need to be able to tolerate this not knowing, this negative capability so that – in the words of Keats (1817) – they are then 'capable of being in uncertainties, mysteries and doubts' in life. The way through this is to become more rooted in your own experience, trusting the wisdom that is there to reveal the way and give up on the illusion of control. This you can do by practising the exercises contained within this book. Indeed that is what they are all designed for: enabling you and your organization to become more anchored and grounded in who you actually are so that from that place you can, with ease, navigate your way more successfully into any unknown and mysteriously emerging future.

Roads to resilience

The Roads to Ruin research has since been followed up by a further study called *Roads to Resilience*, undertaken by Cranfield University on behalf of Airmic (Cranfield School of Management executive briefing (2013) results reproduced with the kind permission of Airmic). Eight leading companies were researched, all of whom had one thing in common: namely, that they constantly had to deal with significant uncertainty and risk and yet have survived, maintaining both reputation and balance sheet. These included AIG, Drax Power, InterContinental Hotels Group, Jaguar Land Rover, Olympic Delivery Authority, The Technology Partnership, Virgin Atlantic and Zurich Insurance.

The findings showed that the sample companies leveraged familiar organizational factors, such as 'leadership', 'people' and 'culture':

> However, they do so in an interconnected way which recognises the changing nature of the business environment, the company's vision for a better world, and, in particular, the passion, motivation and wisdom of people working for the company. (Tomorrow's Good Governance Forum, 2013)

The research found some key principles that were common to all:

- exceptional radar within and beyond the organization;
- strong relationships internally and externally;
- respected and respectful leaders;
- an ability to respond rapidly; and
- diversified resources.

> What links the Roads to Ruin and this new research is the central role executives play in building and sustaining strong and productive relationships, based on mutual trust, respect and inclusion, with customers, employees, shareholder, investors and other key stakeholders, which over time develop into loyalty and contribute to resilience. (Cranfield School of Management/Airmic, 2013)

Wake-up call

You need to decide if you are willing to make the path by walking it. No one can require you to do this. However, failure to do so may mean that you get swept along unconsciously in the old or at best the current organizational reality (see Figure 2.1 on page 25) and no business or organization can succeed or operate at its best if its people continue to behave in this fashion.

This book is a wake-up call inviting you to take up your role in helping to develop the enlightened and resilient organization. The invitation is simply to become more fully conscious of the part that you play in co-creating the whole and to become more accountable for what it is that you can provide in your role. The models and tools contained within the remainder of this book will enable you to develop the skills required to walk the path.

KEY POINTS

1 The role of leadership and followership is changing considerably in the face of increasing uncertainty and change.

2 Traditional 'solo performer' competencies will no longer work within the new organizational structures that are emerging and indeed may have been significantly related to some large and recent corporate failures.

3 New skills are required. These include the ability to be able to embody and defend purpose, work with interconnectedness, build relationship capability, enable change, use conflict as a resource and let go of knowing.

4 Emotional intelligence is a key core competency because if you can learn to trust in your own experience you will be able then to connect with and guide others and in so doing release previously untapped resources within the organization.

5   Resilient organizations succeed, in part, through the passion, motivation and wisdom of their people.

6   Potential leaders and managers need to wake up to the call.

PART TWO
The personal and the interpersonal

Ways in
Theories of the unconscious as a resource

04

"Who looks outside, dreams. Who looks inside, awakens.

CARL JUNG

My role, as an organizational psychologist, is to help create a working environment that supports the people working within it to operate at their very best and to flourish. There are two distinct elements to this. First, understanding what motivates people in their role, how they can best utilize their strengths and talents, and how they can work more effectively with others. I will address this within Part 2 and Chapters 4–7. Second, it involves making sure that the structures and processes within the organization support that understanding and enable people to be able to give of their very best. That means paying attention to issues such as leadership, culture, communication and recognition and reward, which I will look at later in Parts 3 and 4. Both need attention, hence my two-pronged approach.

In this chapter, I will introduce some key theories about motivation and what drives people's performance at a personal and interpersonal level. This is the first prong. The theories will give you some understanding of the nature of being human – an area that is both complex and mysterious. I will look at psychology in terms of the mind, neuroscience in terms of the body and interconnectedness in terms of the heart. This provides the ground for Chapters 5, 6 and 7 where we will explore, more specifically, how you yourself operate in practice, how you relate in a working environment with others and how well you perform when working within the context of a group.

Psychology and the mind

Lawyers, I suppose, were children once. (Charles Lamb)

When working with an individual client I will often be asked to help them develop a new skill or area of competency. They will have realized that they need to develop this skill if they are to be able to perform better in their current or future role. Let me describe a simple example. Say I am working with a client – a lawyer – who, while incredibly intelligent and bright, has difficulty in engaging and motivating their team. This is affecting the performance of the whole group, and ultimately my client's prospects for promotion. I introduce them to a framework or model such as De Bono's Six Thinking Hats (1985), which distinguishes between different ways of operating in life and making decisions (see Figure 4.1).

Preference

Like many psychological frameworks, the model works on the premise that we have, in life, developed a preference for certain ways of being, which have become a habit. They have become useful and efficient ways of operating for us, but may be also limited, at times, if other ways of being then become unavailable to us. To understand preferences, try the following exercise.

EXERCISE 4.1 Preference

- Take a piece of plain paper and a pen.

- Write your full name with your non-dominant hand.

- Now write it with the other hand.

- What is the difference?

- What did you notice? Did it take more time with the non-dominant hand? Was it awkward? Did the quality suffer?

FIGURE 4.1 De Bono's six thinking hats

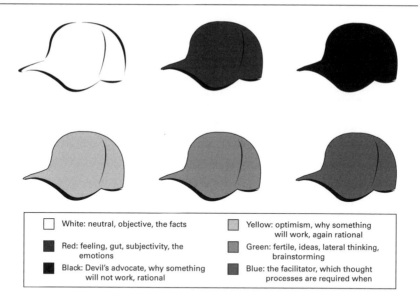

	White: neutral, objective, the facts		Yellow: optimism, why something will work, again rational
	Red: feeling, gut, subjectivity, the emotions		Green: fertile, ideas, lateral thinking, brainstorming
	Black: Devil's advocate, why something will not work, rational		Blue: the facilitator, which thought processes are required when

In the discussion with the client we uncover that they have razor sharp skills in terms of black and white thinking (see Figure 4.1). This is understandable, bearing in the mind the profession that they have chosen and the amount of practice that they will have had, as a lawyer, honing these particular skills. However, what also surfaces in the discussion, is the extent to which they have a restricted palette in terms of the other colours and how much the reds and yellows are less familiar or available to them. We look at the significance of this in terms of how they operate with team members. Then we design specific actions and ways of being that they can then adopt in order to build their capacity for using these 'new' colours. Initially, this might feel unfamiliar and awkward for them and they will not get it right first time. But with practice, feedback and support they can become as automatically skilled at this as they have become with the black and white. In that respect, it's like going through the stages involved in learning to drive (see Figure 4.2).

I find it helpful to use models and frameworks, as a way of illustrating preferences, and as a lens or compass to point towards an idea or concept, and in that way shed more light and understanding. However, people are infinitely more complex than any framework might

FIGURE 4.2   Learning to drive

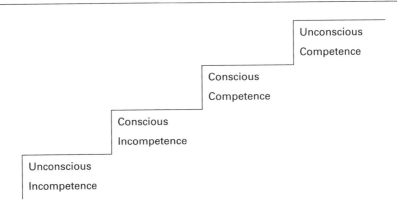

allow. Please, therefore, do treat these models as a kind of map with which to aid understanding of the topography and do not confuse them with the actual territory itself.

The unconscious

Sigmund Freud, a medical doctor and the founder of psychoanalysis, took the view that human beings are motivated to satisfy their own needs and desires as follows:

- safety/security/belonging;
- attention/being seen and met;
- being separate/own person/will;
- autonomy/compliance/rebellion; and
- to love/experience one's desire.

He popularized the notion of the unconscious as the seat of our higher potential and the source of all our real creativity. As a concept, the unconscious had been explored in much of the 19th-century literature. What Freud did though, in the early 20th century, was to demonstrate ways in which it could be made more accessible. We will come back to this in the later chapters of Part 2. Meanwhile, let me continue with the theory. Freud suggested that if your needs, as described above, were met, then you would be free to fully express your creativity and your higher and, heretofore, potential self. According to his theories, a kind of psychological birth takes place, during the early stages of life, and at a time when these needs would ideally have been met for us as children. Then, how we express ourselves later in life, as an adult, will have been fundamentally shaped by the feelings, meaning and sense of identity that we formed in those early years. He used the notion of an iceberg to depict this state (see Figure 4.3).

It gets more complicated because Freud also thought that we are all hardwired for what he called the 'pleasure/pain' principle, meaning that we always seek to have our needs met and to avoid pain. This, regardless of what might be required of the situation. It seems also that we have a deep-seated resistance to change because change, as an unknown quantity, raises our levels of anxiety and, therefore, discomfort or pain. This thinking ties in with the transition curve described in Chapter 1.

Of course, the reality is that none of us will have had all of our needs met in childhood. Freud believed that we were fundamentally shaped by that experience, including any deficits. He believed that our unmet needs or desires and otherwise painful memories from that period are repressed and remain in our unconscious along with our real creativity but that repression does not get rid of them. They instead remain there as determinants of behaviours in the future.

Melanie Reizes Klein was an Austrian born British psychoanalyst and a contemporary of Freud's. Unlike Freud, who had worked with adults, Klein studied infants and very young children during their

FIGURE 4.3 Freud's iceberg

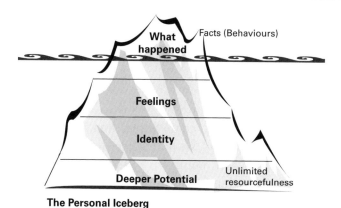

The Personal Iceberg

developing years. From her observations, she concluded that we are primarily social beings, motivated by relational needs. Her attachment theories focus on the infant child's primary relationship with its mother (usually the prime carer) and the manner in which the child's inner world is fundamentally split between love, on the one hand, and fear on the other. She also believed that the child's perception of its external world was split, consisting of two part-objects: a good part of the mother that feeds and comforts it and a bad part of the mother that denies it food and comfort.

Again, none of us will have had our needs met all of the time by a good mother. Klein believed, that as a direct result of our experience in this first primary relationship, we will have developed a pattern of relating which will have become our default script. This script is coloured by these early experiences, which may be located more or less at any point along a scale of acceptance and rejection.

Defences against anxiety

According to these theorists, two things can, therefore, happen to us in our development as a person and our relationship to life. First, having been shaped by our first experience of family and relationships, we will have developed a 'known template' of our self, of others and of the world; a fixed pattern of relating that worked for us back then and strategies for how to try to have our needs met in the world, and therefore how best, we think, to relate, respond or react to the other. Second, in an attempt to avoid pain or anxiety from any unknown other, we will have developed unconscious defences that are designed to safeguard our self from any more harm, in terms of, say, rejection or frustration, whatever are our primary fears. This is because these responses, if experienced in the 'here and now' from the other, might trigger the enormous pain that we had first experienced earlier in our life when, as a child, we were rejected or frustrated. Defences are, therefore, designed to have us avoid dealing with the raw, sensitive, immature and underdeveloped aspects of our selves.

Defences against anxiety are, at the same time, defences against the reality of the 'here and now', so that when an external situation or other presents a stress too painful to bear, we regress to a form of primitive psychic defence mechanism. In doing so, we hope to avoid painful feelings such as anxiety, shame, guilt or vulnerability.

Repression and denial

What are these defences? Well, repression is of itself a major defence against anxiety, as is denial, which we looked at earlier. If we look at some of the case studies referred to in Chapter 2, there was an enormous amount of repression and denial going on at the senior board levels of some of those organizations. For example, neither of the boards of AIG nor Independent Insurance questioned how their companies were producing such exceptionally and consistently good results. Neither Independent Insurer nor its auditors, nor its actuary nor its regulator, heeded the prevailing market view that their results were 'too good to be true'.

Another example, not included within those case studies was the Royal Bank of Scotland (RBS). Here Fred Goodwin, the CEO, blindly pursued a foreign acquisition that was to ultimately bankrupt the bank in 2009. It transpired that little or no due diligence or commercial investigation on the target acquisition had been undertaken. Instead, perhaps, guided by feelings of invincibility and success, Fred Goodwin might conceivably have blindly and recklessly led the bank to its collapse.

'It's not happening' seemed to be the reactive response of many of these senior leaders. Why? Because they could not tolerate the anxiety of being present to what was actually going wrong; to being vulnerable; to experiencing feelings of guilt or shame; or to being with the uncertainty of the situation and therefore simply not knowing? Nor can we confidently blame any one of them individually because the tricky thing, of course, is that because these defence mechanisms operate at the level of our unconscious, they might have been almost totally unaware of what they were doing.

It is for this reason that it is so important for each one of us to shed light on these blind and reactive patterns of response and to try to understand them more fully because otherwise it can become almost impossible for us to lead and manage our organizations in a healthy and successful way.

Splitting

Splitting is another defence mechanism where, as with Klein's earlier dichotomy of good breast and bad breast, we learn to split the world into good guys and bad guys. An example of this might be the 'banker bashing' that arose after the financial crash in the Western world in 2008. People picked on the bankers almost exclusively, perhaps because they could not tolerate the complexity of the situation and their own partial collusion. It is easier to find someone else to blame – the bad bankers – so that we can stay good.

This might also have been part of the problem at RBS. RBS 'won' the acquisition after a battle with Barclays Bank. Often, following these corporate skirmishes, the winner comes away feeling victorious and therefore 'good', making the other failed contestant 'bad'. Did RBS do little or no due diligence after that because as the 'good' party it was after all destined to succeed? This splitting into rather infantile dichotomies might well have stopped them from appreciating the complexity of the deal and ultimately, that it was actually bad and would bring them down.

Projection

Projection is one of the major obstacles to developing a real relationship with the other. It is a defence mechanism that is very prevalent in the workplace and, in my experience, one that is very little understood. Ferenczi, another contemporary of Freud's and Klein's, believed that an infant is inclined to make pleasant experiences part of their own self – termed introjection (see below) while those that are painful are wished away – projected. According to him, people grow up then transferring these repressed feelings onto others.

Simple projection occurs when a person unconsciously attributes to another person a characteristic or feeling that is in fact their own. Let's say, for example, I dislike my CEO. In fact, I dislike them and I am angry with them. These feelings are difficult for me to tolerate because I have to work with my CEO and, seeking pleasure over pain, it is unsettling to have these complex feelings. It would be so much easier if, instead, I could like and admire them. I am not aware of this dramatic tension or conflict going on within me but I have a knee jerk defence mechanism which is brilliant. I transfer or project my uncomfortable feelings onto the CEO. So now my sense of reality becomes the CEO does not like me. In fact, the CEO is angry with me. Subject and object have changed. Because I am totally unaware of what I have done, I now really believe this to be the truth and I act accordingly, in the context of a CEO who I 'know' dislikes me and is even angry with me.

This may lead to awkward or defensive behaviour on my part, which might in turn actually lead the CEO to disliking me or becoming irritated or angry in my presence. My prophesy is then fulfilled, and I have actually created this new distorted 'reality'. Paradoxically, it is easier for me to tolerate these feelings of dislike and anger when they are outside of me, in the CEO, than if they were within me, as part of my own complex internal state. But of course, they are still within me. I have done nothing to change that. Instead, there is a lot of energy wasted between us in blurring the boundaries between who I am and who they really are; what I am feeling and what they are feeling; all of which is wasted because it stops us from being in a real relationship with one another and therefore getting on more effectively with the task.

Introjection

Introjection might be where my boss accepts the feelings that I have projected onto them, say of anger or dislike. Why would the CEO accept these feelings? Well maybe because it is easier to operate as a CEO that is angry than one who is able to be intimate or is vulnerable. It will depend on their template from childhood as to which projections they feel comfortable assuming and which they do not but, of course, more often than not, they will be completely unaware that they are taking on these feelings, which are in fact yours.

Introjections can relate to positive as well as negative feelings. Let's take again, for example, the cases of RBS and Enron. Perhaps the board members, senior people at both organizations, relevant stakeholders (such as Arthur Andersen, the lending banks in the case of Enron and the rating agencies for both) projected feelings of omnipotence and infallible leadership onto their leaders, because they themselves were at some level uncomfortable with the complexity and uncertainty of the market and needed to feel more secure. Then Fred Goodwin, the CEO at RBS, and Ken Lay, the Enron chairman, might have happily interjected these projections, feeling themselves then to be actually omnipotent and infallible. This type of unconscious collusion would have disabled any real challenge or debate within both companies and stopped them from having the type of courageous conversations that needed to be had if they were to reverse the downward trajectory of both businesses.

A resource

This may all sound rather pathological but often pathological behaviour is only an extreme form of the behaviour of a normal person, and neurotic (anxiety that derives from the self) behaviour, one of degree not kind. But there is hope because underneath all of this pathology there is the possibility for tremendous growth and development. That was what Freud and his contemporaries were seeking to do, help transform people by working with the unconscious. We are none of us perfect. We are instead human with unmet drives and needs and, if we can be accepting of that truth, we will be able to be much more present to what is actually going on. If we want to be able to see more clearly and work with interconnectedness then we have to lift the veils of awareness and get real about our own attitudes, behaviours and emotional, and at times reactive, responses in life and work. This is what lies at the heart of EQ, the key core competency that we looked at in Chapter 3.

If our unconscious carries our untapped creativity, as well as the roots of some of our pain, then it also offers the seeds for our success. If we can have the strength of character to be with some of that anxiety and pain, that is when we will be able to free up the source of our real creativity and our greater potential in life. By making the decision to do this personal work, we can free up our 'passion, motivation and wisdom', qualities that were discovered to be distinguishing critical factors in the Roads to Resilience research referred to in Chapter 3. This untapped potential is the very resource that is needed to free us up to do great things, and we are wasting far more energy on trying to keep it contained and suppressed than we would need for the completion of any great work. The answers to the challenge of our times will increasingly come from this deep place, not outside, as Jung says, 'in dreams'.

We are normal. We are human. Work with that fact consciously and you will be on the right path. To quote the words of Leonard Cohen, 'There is a crack in everything, that's how the light gets in...' (2011). So you do not need to do, or become something different – you simply need to become more conscious of what is already there. That of itself will enable you to see more clearly, be more effective in your decision making and more real and connected in your relationship with others. Lao Tse said, 'The snow goose need not bathe to make itself white. Neither need you do anything but be yourself'.

Neuroscience and the body

> Mr Duffy lived a short distance from his body. (James Joyce)

Freud and his contemporaries showed us how the mind can have an enormous influence on our attitudes, behaviour and performance at work. So too is there wisdom to be gleaned from what goes on in our bodies – that is, if we pay attention to it. In which case, it too, can become an enormously rich resource for us. This involves the discipline of neuroscience, a school of thought that adopts an evolutionary approach to our development. It begins, not with childhood as above, but instead millions of years ago and indeed with the start of all life forms on earth.

Two brains

According to this view our bodies and brains are set up to respond emotionally to things. What complicates matters is that we have two different sets of brains. An old primitive one that we share with many other animals such as dogs and monkeys, and that has the capacity for primary emotions such as anger, anxiety, disgust, joy or fun. In our old brain we have basic defensive behaviours. We can attack if angry, run away if anxious or become very submissive if meeting something more powerful than ourselves in terms of status. My dog can also do these things. Even animals that live in the sea, such as dolphins, behave in this fashion – and many are also motivated to achieve similar things to us, including close social relationships.

Then, about two million years ago, the human brain evolved a number of abilities for thinking in new ways. We became able to imagine and fantasize about things; to think, to reason and to plan in ways that other animals cannot. We developed a consciousness and sense of self. Unlike other animals, we can think about the future and the kind of self we want to be, about how we want to feel and the life we want to live, whereas other animals live primarily from day to day. As humans, we can look back on events in the past with regret. We can ruminate about unhappy things from either the past or the future. These new abilities are referred to as being part of our new brain.

Problems arise because our new brain abilities can get hijacked by our old brain defence mechanisms, so that our planning, reasoning, imagining or ruminating becomes directed by the primal emotions and motives of the old brain. Then, rather than using our thinking and attention to control unpleasant emotions or to help us to stimulate positive emotions, the old brain instead pulls us in the direction of threat-based anxiety and fear, and this then becomes the focus of our thinking, feeling and imagining (see Figure 4.4).

It's not your fault

One of my mediation teachers, Rob Nairn, always emphasizes the point that none of this is our fault and that it is as true for you as it is for me and, indeed, every person on the planet. It is simply something that is a part of our physical make-up and difficult to automatically override, but we can loosen its grip by doing a little work. If we can trip the switch somehow, we might then instead be able to use our new brains to develop increased consciousness about what is actually happening to us at any point in time. This means using our new brains consciously to see more clearly what is actually going on. With this increased level of awareness and consciousness we can then make

FIGURE 4.4 The evolved brain

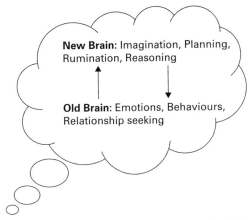

SOURCE *Mindful Compassion*, Gilbert and Choden (2013) Reproduced with the kind permission of Choden

choices about more appropriate ways of responding. Exercise 3.1 (page 44) is designed to develop that capacity for self-regulation. It will enable you to notice, label, feel and, with the slight distance that has then been created, develop choices about how best to behave. In this way we begin to redirect our otherwise primitive hardwiring and knee-jerk patterns of response. We can be in the present, for as Eckhart Tolle helpfully suggests: 'Nothing has happened in the past; it happened in the Now. Nothing will ever happen in the future; it will happen in the Now'. (*The Power of Now*, 1999)

Emotional regulation

Neuroscience research has revealed that we have three types of emotional regulation systems, each of which is designed to do different things (Depue and Morrone-Strupinsky, 2005; LeDoux, 1998; Panksepp, 1998; Gilbert and Choden, 2013). These systems are depicted, as parts of the whole in Figure 4.5. Understanding them will help you to see how you might be able to trip the switch and use your new brain to control your old brain, rather than the other way around.

Threat system

The function of this system is to pick up on threats quickly. It gives us bursts of feelings such as anxiety, anger or disgust, which then travel instantly throughout our bodies, alerting us to take immediate action

FIGURE 4.5   The three systems

SOURCE *Mindful Compassion*, Gilbert and Choden (2013) Concept reproduced with the kind permission of Choden

to protect ourselves against the threat. Although this system can be the source of painful and difficult feelings, it is ultimately designed to protect us, as it did our ancestors when faced, for example, with a lion or tiger in the jungle.

The threat system does not take time out to ponder or think; it can't, when faced with a tiger and the choice of life and death. Instead, it reacts immediately and automatically on the principle that time is of the essence and that it is better to be safe and alive, than sorry and dead. This system is also very easily triggered and activated because it is primarily designed for self-protection. All of which explains why, in facing a perceived threat at work – take our boss as a modern-day example of the tiger – we might react very quickly and in an overly defensive way, somewhere between the polarities of fight (argue with the boss) and flight (retreat and sulk).

Drive system

The function of this system is to give us positive feelings that then motivate and encourage us to seek out situations and resources that we need in order to survive and flourish in life. When balanced with the other two systems it can lead us towards important goals, such as passing an exam, getting that promotion or falling in love. It releases a substance in our brain called *dopamine*, which gives us feelings of success that, from an evolutionary point of view, indicate that things are going well. It also gives us the impetus to enjoy and keep seeking these situations out because they not only give us pleasure but also get us what we need and want in life. Imagine how dull life would be without these feelings; where, instead, you had little motivation, energy or desire. So all good so far and, as we saw in Chapter 3 with the Roads to Resilience case studies, the organizations where people have this kind of energy, as a resource available to them and others, are also the ones that are more likely to be resilient and successful.

However, the problem is that this system can also become over-stimulated, leading us into just wanting more and more. So that, ultimately, when we cannot satisfy this unquenchable thirst for pleasure, we begin instead to experience feelings of frustration and disappointment. It can allow our old brain to take over the attention, thinking and planning faculties of our new brain. This means that, for example, while we know at some level that more food, drink, exercise or work are not required, we want and have more anyway. This can really play out in a goal-orientated organization where people are encouraged to just seek more and more; to do more and more; to be more and more perfectionist. This without any real discernment about whether this 'doing' is appropriate or not, bearing in mind the objectives of the task and the overall purpose of the organization. In this type of working environment, people are encouraged to mindlessly seek out opportunities and achievement in a way that ultimately becomes relentless and exhausting. This might explain, in part, the reckless drive behaviour that characterized some of the case studies in the Roads to Ruin research that is referred to in Chapter 2.

Soothing system

This third system enables us to bring a sense of peacefulness to our bodies and minds, which restores our balance. When animals are not defending themselves against threats and problems, and don't need to achieve or do anything because they have enough, then they can just rest and be content. Contentment is a form of being happy with the way things are, and feeling safe. It describes an inner state of peacefulness that is altogether different from striving or wanting. When people practice meditation and other ways of slowing down, these are the feelings that they report: not wanting or striving but instead feeling calmer inside, stiller and more connected to others.

This system releases endorphins that stimulate these feelings of calmness and connection and, in particular, *oxytocin*, which promotes feelings of social safeness and affiliation. The system is also referred to as the parasympathetic system and relates closely to some of Klein's work and how 'soothing' it is for us to receive affection and kindness from others. Mother's bodies, when they give birth, become flooded with *oxytocin*, thought to be to boost the social bonding with their new-born child.

The question that arises, as you will see in Exercise 5.7 on page 89, is how much time you allow for yourself to be in this system. In many organizations, people can feel anxious when they spend too much time in the soothing system. It is as if the drive system kicks in and makes them feel guilty about not doing or achieving something. By contrast, some more enlightened organizations take steps to ensure that their people spend time here. That is because they know the real value of rebalancing from this place and the tangible benefits that are derived in terms of wellness and people being able to see more clearly, be more discerning and therefore make better decisions and, of course, the critical skill for our new reality, form better working relationships with other.

Some businesses, such as Google, invite the Buddhist monk, Thich Nhat Hanh in to integrate 'lazy days' into people's busy schedules. In that vein, many of the exercises in this part are equally designed to help bring you into this parasympathetic system. The theory being that paradoxically by letting go, by slowing down, by being in the soothing system and noticing what is happening in your body, all manner of new insights and ideas can reveal themselves to you. It is, therefore, potentially a tremendous resource to you in your work. It allows for a deeper level of knowing to surface and ultimately enables a more discerning, successful and enlightened organization to emerge. This state is fundamentally about being, not doing.

Hardwired

Again none of this is your fault. We are all simply hardwired from an evolutionary perspective to operate from our more primitive brain functions. Yet, as we evolve so does our consciousness. We know now, for example, that if we pay attention to balancing these three systems, our decision making and performance will improve, as will the success of our impact on our organization and the world.

The exercises in Chapters 5–7 will address all three of the systems but it is worth pointing out that one of the key 'ways in' to seeing what is going on within any one of them is through our bodies. Maybe meditation, maybe dance, maybe walking. The methodology does not really matter. Simple, focused attention on our bodies and what is actually going on there can be a complete revelation, offering clues and insights into what is going on outside that could not otherwise have been arrived at. The feeling in the gut at a meeting, the pain in the back, the fluttering in the heart are all often signals of what needs attending to outside. In that way, the body has its own way of knowing. This, of course, is great news if we learn to attend to it and use it as a resource.

Interconnectedness and the heart

> Your great mistake is to act the drama as if you were alone. (David Whyte)

In this chapter we have looked at theories about what motivates and drives people to perform. Can we now extrapolate from that something about their organizations? Can we, by looking at individuals and how they operate, in some way predict or make a hypothesis about how their organization is likely to behave? Larry Hirschhorn (1991) believes that we can make such predictions and that 'there will be a resonance in them of the emotional experience of the organization as a system and the emotional undertow of dealings with and from the outside'. It is as if one is affecting the other, much like the resonance between the two prongs of my tuning fork, in the two-pronged approach. Siegmund Foulkes and James Anthony (1965), like many other theorists operating post two world wars, put forward the view that in any organization there will be a group consciousness that then shapes and determines the behaviour of the group as a whole. They write:

> The network of all individual and mental processes, the psychological medium in which they meet, communicate, and interact can be called the matrix ... In further formulation of our observations we have come to conceive these processes not merely as interpersonal but transpersonal.

The new sciences

Maybe we are not alone, as we might have thought. Indeed, many theorists would argue about the notion of separateness. They suggest that we are all interconnected at a very deep level and, certainly, the financial crisis has forced a paradigm shift in an understanding of interconnectedness and how it plays out between retail and investment banking, between governments globally, between governments and the financial sector, between financial services and the media, and between the lender and the borrower. Maybe the illusion of separateness is no longer sustainable.

So too, the thinking goes at the juncture of the perceived boundaries between the modern sciences. For example, in terms of the social sciences, we clearly no longer live in separate communities unaffected by one another. Then quantum physics is opening up our understanding of the links between the very small and the very large. The concept of the 'Holon' is helpful here, where the part reflects the essence of the whole; for example, the holographic plate, from every fragment of which the whole image may be recovered. I will revisit this idea of the Holon in later chapters and, in particular, in Parts 3 and 4, where we will look in detail at how the whole and the parts operate within organizational systems.

Scientists are also discovering how the universe seems to consist of two elements – energy and consciousness – where particles all influence each other and thereby ultimately the whole. And new exciting ideas about chaos, randomness and a deeper ordering and patterning to everything are emerging, for example the 'butterfly effect'. The writer Ray Bradbury and Edward Lorenz, a meteorologist, drew attention to this by showing how the flap of a butterfly in Tokyo could affect a tornado in Texas (or a thunderstorm in New York). We see the same patterns of affective behaviour within organizations. One casual remark at a meeting or flippant gesture can fly through the organization, growing and mutating into a huge misunderstanding that then requires enormous effort and time and energy to resolve.

Chaos theories are suggesting a new ordering, as if, somehow, abrupt and violent change in nature might, at times, be necessary for our planetary survival. There are strong links here with the illusion of control that I referred to in Chapter 1 and how some organizations and businesses can come to see themselves as invincible; their leaders and managers unable to let go. They can develop a sense of entitlement to life/success and survival that belies the true reality of the world that we live in. Margaret Wheatley (1993) puts it thus:

> Chaos's role in the emergence of new order is so well-known that it seems strange that Western culture had denied its part so vehemently. In the dream of dominion over all nature, we believed we could eliminate chaos from life. We believed there were straight lines to the top. If we set a goal or claimed a vision, we would get there, never looking back, never forced to descend into confusion or despair. Those beliefs led us far from life, far from the processes by which newness is created. And it is only now, as modern life grows ever more turbulent and control slips away, that we are willing again to contemplate chaos. Whether we

explore its dynamics through new science or ancient myths, the lesson is important. The destruction created by chaos is necessary for the creation of anything new.

Universal consciousness and the call

The spirit of inquiry between the new sciences and spiritual studies of consciousness opens us up again to ideas of part and whole as well as chaos and uncertainty. However, it also opens us up to the idea of an underlying order and to that which is intrinsically knowable by us. Spirituality, in this sense, recognizes that each individual is a unique but integral and in some ways an undifferentiated part of a larger system, with a unique evolutionary path and purpose in service of the whole. From this perspective, spiritual wisdom is inherently systemic, pointing to one infinite system in which all is interconnected. We will look at systems theory in more detail in Chapter 8.

Jung, a psychoanalyst and contemporary of Freud's, popularized the notion of a collective unconscious and the unique creative potential of each of us. He coined the term 'individuation', by which he meant the lifelong development process through which a person works towards development of their inherent self. This begs questions about the meaning, purpose and values implicit in the evolutionary path of human beings. Why are we here? For what purpose? Why am I here? Why this organization? What is my part in the whole? Am I fulfilling a calling or purpose within the whole of creation that is simply beyond my rational comprehension? For Jung, 'the decisive question for a man is: is he related to something infinite or not?'

The lens of interconnectedness highlights how the illusion of separateness can cause us to waste energy in defensive patterns of response. Even, perhaps, more importantly it demonstrates how we look at life and the challenges that we face from our own small, personal and separate perspective, rather than from the perspective of the whole, which by its very nature is more infinite and whole. We look at our challenges from inside of ourselves and in a way that is often needy and personal, rather than from the outside context that we find ourselves in, and a place that has infinitely more resources than just our own. It raises questions then about where we should be placing our attention: in ourselves, falsely, as the centre of everything and in control; or outside, looking at the broader reality as it actually is, complex and impermanent, and then from this place seeing what the context might actually require from us and our organization going forward.

Integration

The conceptual separation between mind, body and spirit or heart is of course misleading. No single model or conceptual scheme embraces the whole breadth and complexity of reality, although each in turn may be useful as a way in to understanding yourself in role. With Freud and the mind we discovered the power and potential of the unconscious. We saw how it can be a tremendous resource but also trip us up without our even noticing. With neuroscience and the body, we saw how important it was to pay attention to all three emotional regulation systems and in a humbling kind of way how close we are, in reality, to the animal kingdom. With interconnectedness and the heart, we saw the bigger picture and the search for self. Viktor Frankyl (1959) says that our greatest motivation in life 'is not to gain pleasure or to avoid pain, but rather to see meaning'.

All three disciplines suggest an evolutionary path that is helped greatly by paying attention to what is actually happening in your own experience in the here and now. You can then, with this new awareness, walk the path more meaningfully from that place. The next three chapters will help you to do this.

KEY POINTS

1 We are not rational beings, as science and philosophy might have previously suggested.

2 We have an unconscious mind that is not accessible by rational means and that causes us to behave in emotional and reactive ways. However, if accessed and understood, the unconscious can

prove to be a tremendous resource in that it allows for a deeper level of knowing to emerge.

3. The view from psychology is that therein lies the source of our true potential, as well as our pain and anxiety, and that unconscious defences against anxiety get in the way of our performing at our best.

4 The view from neuroscience is that we need to pay attention to our bodies, balancing our three distinct emotional systems, and work to stop our primitive brain responses from impacting on us in role.

5 The view from theories about interconnectedness suggest a bigger systemic picture and one where connection is a given and meaning is the call.

6 An integrated path suggests lifting the veils of awareness by paying more attention to your own actual experience in the here and now and by this route getting to see your own attitudes, behaviours and responses and how these impact on you in role. Then, using this insight as a resource to inform you in your work. This is what lies at the heart of EQ, the key core competency that we looked at in Chapter 3.

7 Developing more conscious awareness will free up your untapped resources as well as your passion, purpose and potency, which will then improve your decision making and performance as well as the success of your impact on your organization and the world.

Ways into self
Me

05

> *Our deepest fear is not that we are inadequate. Our deepest fear is that we are powerful beyond measure. It is our light, not our darkness, that most frightens us. We ask ourselves, 'Who am I to be brilliant, gorgeous, talented, fabulous?' Actually, who are you not to be? You are a child of God. Your playing small does not serve the world. There is nothing enlightened about shrinking so that other people won't feel insecure around you. We are all meant to shine, as children do.* **MARIANNE WILLIAMSON, SPOKEN BY NELSON MANDELA AT HIS INAUGURATION IN 1994**

I hope that you will appreciate, by this stage of the book, your own fundamental importance in terms of adding value to your organization and building something greater in the world. Furthermore, that in order to do this you need to be able and willing to open up to your real potential in life and to operate effectively within the context that you find yourself in, working to purpose and in role. This chapter addresses all of these issues.

As we saw in the last chapter with Carl Jung 'Who looks outside dreams. Who looks inside awakens', this notion of realizing self is not new. Indeed, it is age-old wisdom. However, it is becoming increasingly relevant in the context of the current business environment because of the changing paradigms, referred to in the earlier chapters in Part 1. We are none of us cocooned any longer within a hierarchical structure, where the company strategy is robust, and the way ahead fairly certain and clear; where we could have been directed, if we had wanted, by external events and effectively been told what to do, and who to be by our managers and leaders. Instead, we now increasingly, whether we want to or not, form part of a mobile and interconnected future paradigm. In this place, the context is changing and uncertain and the path ahead unclear. From here, we operate within a diverse network of relationships needing to collaborate within and across organizational structures that have semi-permeable boundaries. We increasingly need to take responsibility for our own actions, and for what is required of us in our role within the immediate and present context of the business. Self-authorization, accountability and the ability to be able to respond appropriately to situations as they arise, change and evolve is now part of the day job, because a successful and emerging strategy can only be implemented through our co-creation.

You may well find that organizational rules and norms need to be interpreted, reinterpreted and sometimes even reinvented and that, as a leader or manager, you need to trust more in and rely increasingly upon your own values and judgements to do this successfully. This undoubtedly involves bringing more of your person or self to the role and yet, as we saw in Chapter 4, doing this can also be difficult because it can surface personal feelings, possibly of vulnerability, uncertainty and anxiety.

Developing more awareness of self enables us to assess our values and purpose, to monitor and adjust our thoughts and to learn to trust our emotions, using them in a way that serves us in fulfilling this more complex role within the business. It enables us to develop an ability to respond (*response ability*) to situations and events rather than reacting to them. In addition, it provides the space for real discernment in the face of the varied challenges and opportunities that present and leads paradoxically to a situation where, by knowing our self more intimately, we also become more deeply connected in our relationships with others.

Sometimes this spirit of inquiry about self will lead us to make small adjustments or tweaks in our behaviour, and at other junctures larger adjustments may be required. In that respect, there will always be seasons for things. The issue really is that it is important for us to take responsibility for making sure that we are aligning the fit between the business and what might be required of us in our roles and for realizing our given talents and potential in the world and in so doing helping to add real value to the business.

Ultimately who you are being will be critical in your role because in a flatter networked structure there is absolutely no place for a leader or manager to hide. What you say and do in front of others, both internally and externally, can increasingly have huge significance in terms of your overall impact on the business.

Some tools and techniques

What can help greatly is having some tools and techniques and a framework to work with, in the face of this complexity. The 'Grounding Steps' framework (see Figure 5.1) will root you within your purpose and core strengths while also enabling you to remain open, flexible, discerning and able to act. In this chapter, I will cover a range of tools and techniques that you can use during the different stages of the Grounding Steps framework.

The exercises are experiential, by which I mean that their value and learning come from the experience of applying them in practice to the unique circumstances of your own individual case. There is the story of the man who read the book on maths and became a mathematician. Then he read a book on physics and became a physicist. Finally, he read a book on swimming and drowned. The point being that the book on swimming could only ever be a guide and the real learning had to take place in the water.

So too it will be with these models and techniques. They are but guides and the real learning and discoveries will take place when you allow them to take you deeply into the water and experience whatever might arise in terms of new insights and discoveries. So it is best if you pick and choose the tools that appeal to you, as you progress through the rest of this book, and starting from where you are, begin to actually apply them for yourself. Some may look deceptively simple and others deceptively complex but don't be fooled by appearances; just try them out. Then you will be more able to:

- understand your purpose and role within the organization;
- keep track of your intention and motivation when working in role;
- see clearly your gifts and where you could meaningfully add value to your organization;

- understand what might be getting in the way of your own success;
- appreciate the differences that others can provide;
- work effectively with others both within and beyond the organization and in an interconnected way;
- learn to see beyond your current limits, thereby also enabling others in the organization to benefit from new insights and resources;
- cultivate the ability to question 'known' reality and to let go of limited ways of being and working;
- become practised at stopping and exercising discernment; and
- learn to let go and allow for new things to emerge and be co-created.

The Grounding Steps framework

The first step of the Grounding Steps framework (see Figure 5.1) is concerned with purpose, the second with insight, the third, openness and the fourth and final step, wisdom. Let's look at each of them in turn.

Step 1: Purpose

It is only with the heart that one can see rightly; what is essential is invisible to the eye. (Antoine de Saint-Exupéry)

When I left school, I was 17. I qualified with good results but was not really sure which path to pursue. I knew that I would go to college but to study what? Computer Science? Languages? Science? Law? How does one choose in the face of multiple options? The answer comes back to knowing one's self – knowing what would give you joy, what would make your heart sing and what has real value and meaning for you. It is this heartfelt knowing that can then help guide such significant choices in life. This first step, purpose, is concerned with building this capacity for knowingness within you; with getting to the heart of what matters to you at any point in time and with being able to remember and stay in touch with that. The means by which you get there is, by and large, irrelevant.

FIGURE 5.1 The Grounding Steps framework

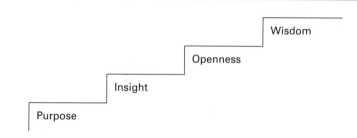

An organization without purpose also flounders, like a sailing boat without a mast. Which direction should it travel in? What course of action should it take? What will happen in rough seas? Similarly, it is vital that you have a deep knowledge of your purpose at work, which can then guide you like a compass when you are trying to steer your organization and, maybe at times, help it to cross rough and difficult seas. This first step, purpose, is concerned with building that capacity for knowing, so that you can get to the heart of what really matters to you and your organization, and stay connected with what has real value and meaning.

People join organizations for all sorts of reasons. Money, security, relationships, a sense of value and belonging, self-esteem, recognition and in order to fulfil one's vocation or potential in life. Do you know why you are involved with the organizations that you currently belong to? Other than money (if you get that), what do you get for yourself from working and being involved there? In an ideal world, you would be there because their purpose in being in the world is very closely aligned with yours. But to be able to say that requires that you first know yours. It is a big question. What is my purpose in life? And not one that you would have to ask yourself every day of the week. However, there are seasons for things, and there will undoubtedly be significant times in your life when you will be required to look at this – perhaps, as I mentioned above, when leaving school or maybe changing jobs or starting a family. Often, too, an event or mid-life crisis can suddenly stop us in our tracks and force us to reassess and evaluate our priorities in life.

In the old paradigm, you might have been able to survive organizational life without looking at these bigger questions. The psychological contract was different then, because the context was more stable and secure. Now, however, it has to become part of the equation that you make with your organization that you can flex and adjust in the face of complexity and change. However, as we have seen from the Roads to Ruin research in Chapter 2, we cannot bob along this complex, changing operating environment without some fixed point of reference to guide our actions. We cannot operate and expand mindlessly, as did some of the organizations that were included in those case studies. This is because, if we do, we may well, like them, suffer at the vagaries of the world outside with little control over our brand and reputation and therefore our destiny. Margaret Wheatley (1993) remarks:

> When chaos has banged down the door and is tossing us around the room, it is difficult to believe that clear principles are sufficient... But if we can trust the workings of the world, we will see that the strength of our organization is maintained if we retain clarity about the purpose and direction of the organization. When things become chaotic, this clarity keeps us on course. We are still able to make sense, even if the world grows mad.

This is why it is so important that you develop and maintain a clear view of who you are in the world and your overall purpose, intention and motivation. It is this that will enable you to make appropriate choices that are aligned with organizational purpose and then better navigate your way through multiple stakeholder relationships. It is this that will provide the glue or centripetal force that will help to keep your networked relationships connected, vibrant and alive.

It will be important socially too. You might, for example, be working increasingly from abroad and in other ways uprooted from your original family environment. Religion and other aspects of community life might play less of a role in your life and your affiliation needs at work may, therefore, be greater than before. It then becomes imperative to develop a strong sense of who you are in the world so that you can, as required, resource and sustain yourself from that place.

Below are some exercises that will help you to discover, or re-evaluate, your purpose in life, as well as the intention and motivation behind the organizations that you chose to involve yourself with, and the decisions that you take in your role.

Exercises 5.1 and 5.2 are taken from the *Age of Unreason* by Charles Handy (1986).

EXERCISE 5.1 Life line

Draw a line to represent your life from birth to death and mark a cross where you are now on that line. Think about it for a bit but not too long; this is an impressionistic exercise not a precise one. Most people will draw a line something like the one below. Do yours before you read on.

FIGURE 5.2 Life line

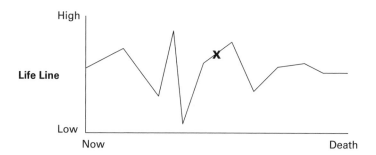

In effect it is a line over time going up and down. What, however, do the ups and downs represent? The answer will tell you something about your real priorities in life. What was significant about your line? What do you think the line says about what matters most to you in life? What are your current priorities? Where did you put the cross? The position will tell you something about the proportion of your life that you still feel is ahead of you. Does the line go upwards at the end or downwards? What might be missing from your future? Are there any adjustments required?

EXERCISE 5.2 Obituary

Write your own obituary to appear in your favourite paper or journal. Assume that it is written by a good friend who knows you well and understands the 'you' behind the facts. Don't write more than 200 words. Perhaps then share it with a close friend.

EXERCISE 5.3 Magic wand

Imagine you have a magic wand and that you can do almost anything with this wand. 'Wave' five things that you would like to have achieved in your life. Suspend judgement or evaluation at this stage and just make them up. What do they look like and feel like? Then assess and choose what specifically you would like to realize and write a detailed description of your ideal outcome.

These three exercises all force you to stand at the end of your life and look backwards. They put what you are doing now into perspective, and force you to work out what you would like to be remembered for. As exercises in very personal re-framing, they paradoxically also free you up to make choices that you might not otherwise have believed possible. This is because standing in the future, you will have already realized your objectives and therefore know, at some deep level, that they are achievable.

Some spiritual disciplines teach that you cannot really live life to the full unless and until you have faced the inevitability of death and, in many ways, these exercises force you to do that. In so doing, they help you to assess what matters most to you right now. This notion of life, death and impermanence is a big theme and one that I think is ultimately about understanding that change is always there. Being anxious about it is a needless waste of energy. Better instead to see impermanence as enabling you to better appreciate what you actually have right now, in the present. My son is nine and I love that. But he won't always be nine and so I am really appreciating that about him right now. Or, in organizational terms, better to use that desired future to inform and appreciate the present.

Let's take Apple as an example of the power of working in this way – from the future. Apple did not set out to sell computers. It wanted to change the world by making information more accessible to all. The computer was simply the means to getting there. This visionary and altruistic cause has shaped every business decision since and is responsible for the almost reverential followers that they attract and the frenzy whipped up in the media every time they speak or deliver a new product. So too with the organizations that were included in the Roads to Resilience research. They each had a company vision for a better world, which helped inform their activities and decision making in the present, making them more resilient and successful over the longer term.

Step 2: Insight

> God grant me the serenity to accept the things I cannot change;
> courage to change the things I can; and wisdom to know the difference.
> (Reinhold Niebuhr)

The second step of the Grounding Steps framework (see Figure 5.1) deals with insight. It is concerned with the extent to which you are aware of the strengths and gifts that you possess and can offer to your organization and the world. We saw in Chapter 4 how we all go through life developing preferences, or ways of operating, that enable us ultimately to become unconsciously competent in certain areas. The aim of this insight step is to shed light on those competencies: your natural and given gifts and strengths.

Insight brings the longer-term focus of purpose in Step 1 into shorter relief and asks us to consider the answers that we came up with at Step 1 from the point of view of our talents and strengths. Let's say, for example, my answers at Step 1 were to help create understanding and ease within organizations or to enable people to be healthy and fit. Step 2 would ask me to consider how my unique gifts and strengths might be deployed in order to best contribute to either of these different paths.

I know that it may sound fairly obvious but when I was 17, and trying to decide which college course to pursue, I had no idea what my real gifts or strengths were. Yes, I had good grades but what did an A in Maths or English tell me about what I might be naturally fluent and good at in the world? It was much later, when having worked successfully as a lawyer, that I discovered some of my more innate and core abilities and, in part, through doing some of the exercises below. You may be much more self-aware, than I was then, but the real value of making these gifts conscious is that you can then align your choices in terms of career and role to things that you love to do naturally. Allowing for greater congruence, in this way, will enable authenticity, creativity and ease. And, as we will see in the next chapter, it will also enable you to work more effectively with others, appreciating the value of the different and complementary strengths that they can provide.

EXERCISE 5.4 Skills list

Imagine yourself asking ten friends – or better still ask ten friends – to list one quality each that they like or admire in you. List those qualities and against each list two activities where those qualities have been useful to you in the past and one type of different activity where they could conceivably be useful in the future.

EXERCISE 5.5 Six thinking hats

As discussed in Chapter 4, Edward De Bono, in *Six Thinking Hats* (1985), describes six preferred ways of thinking.

Looking at the preferences described in Figure 4.1 (page 55)

- Which two colours are you aware of using most of the time?

- Which two colours are your least favourite/used?

- How do you engage with people who prefer your least used colours?

- How might it help you in your role, including your decision making, to use all six?

Personality profiles and Myers Briggs

Some of the tools that an organizational psychologist is qualified to use with clients are what we call psychometrics or personality profiles. These are self-report questionnaires, where the individual client rates themself on a broad range of dispositions and the psychologist then works closely with them to uncover what the pattern of responses indicates about their core strengths and gifts. These tools are statistically valid and reliable predictors of future performance, and therefore used extensively by psychologists in order to help clients develop more insight and awareness. In the hands of a trained expert these tools can be invaluable, enabling the client to appreciate and play into their core strengths at work while also becoming more mindful of potential areas of weakness.

It is beyond the scope of this book to present any of these profiles in great detail. However, I have set out below a synopsis of one such test, called Myers Briggs, which I use a lot in my work. If you are interested in the preferences that it explores then I recommend that you find an expert who is trained to administer it and who can work with you on your profile.

The Myers Briggs personality profile is commonly used within a business context because it is a very accessible way to explore and understand how people differ in their approach to the world and to making decisions. It is a powerful tool for better understanding what motivates you and what unique skills and talents you bring to your role. Based originally on the work of Carl Jung, it distinguishes between four different sets of preferences that go to make up different temperaments (see Figure 5.3).

FIGURE 5.3 Myers Briggs polarities

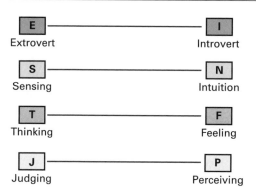

First, people express preferred modes of behaviour somewhere between extroversion (E) and introversion (I). The E person derives energy from contact and interaction with others, while the I person finds such contact tiring and seeks energy from internal reflective sources.

Second, people have a preference along a spectrum that stretches from sensation (S) at one end to intuition (N) at the other. The S person prefers facts and knows and understands life through experience; such a person is firmly anchored in tangible reality that can be seen and

FIGURE 5.4   The four temperaments

The SJ or Epimethean Person

Leadership Style:	Traditionalist, stabilizer, consolidator
Work Style:	Works from a sense of responsibility, loyalty, and industry
Learning Style:	Learns in a step-by-step way with preparation for current and future reality
Contribution:	Timely output

The SP or Dionysian Person

Leadership Style:	Trouble-shooter, negotiator, fire fighter
Work Style:	Works via action with cleverness and timeliness
Learning Style:	Learns through active involvement to meet current needs
Contribution:	Expeditious handling of the out-of-the-ordinary and the unexpected

The NF or Apollonian Person

Leadership Style:	Catalyst, spokesperson, energiser
Work Style:	Works by interacting with people about values and inspirations
Learning Style:	Learns for self-awareness through personalised and imaginative ways
Contribution:	Something personal or a special vision of possibilities

The NT or Promethean Person

Leadership Style:	Visionary, architect of systems, builder
Work Style:	Works on ideas with ingenuity and logic
Learning Style:	Learns by an impersonal and analytical process for personal mastery
Contribution:	Strategies and analyses

measured. The N person lives in anticipation of the future and looks for change, exploring numerous activities all at once and preferring values, subjective knowing and inspiration as a way of experiencing life.

The third pair of preferences is thinking (T) and feeling (F). The T person prefers the logical, impersonal basis for choice, while the F person prefers the personal emotional basis.

Finally, there is the spectrum running from perceiving (P) to judging (J). The P person prefers to keep options open and fluid, seeing things from different points of view, while the J person prefers closure, that is, narrowing choices down and reaching solutions.

As a lawyer, I was using skills that were more inclined towards the polarities of I, S, T, and J. I was good at this but when, much later, I completed the Myers Briggs questionnaire, I discovered that my natural preference was more towards the polarities of E, N, F and P and, ultimately therefore, much more naturally suited to the role I have now, as an organizational psychologist. Had I completed the questionnaire at 17, when leaving school, I wonder what this insight would have meant for me in terms of choices about college courses and beyond?

The four preference pairs lead to 16 possible personality types and these can be sorted into four broad categories or temperaments, as shown in Figure 5.4.

EXERCISE 5.6   Myers Briggs

Mark where you think you would be on each of the four polarities described in Figure 5.3.

- Which of the four temperaments described in Figure 5.4 do you relate to the most?

- Which of the four do you find most difficult to work with?

- What might this mean for you in your role?

- How might it affect your relationship with significant others?

- What do you think most irritates others about your preferences?

Step 3: Openness

> We make ourselves powerless when we choose not to know. But we give
> ourselves hope when we insist on looking. As all wisdom does, seeing
> starts with simple questions: what could I know, should I know, and
> that I don't know? Just what am I missing here? (Margaret Heffernan)

Steps 1 and 2 of the Grounding Steps framework are concerned with
purpose and insight; with what matters and has most meaning for
us and with the specific skills and gifts that we bring to our role
(see Figure 5.1). Doing the relevant exercises above will have enabled
you to see more clearly your purpose in life and in role and to understand and appreciate the natural strengths and talents that you offer
to your organization. This perspective is very much about self and
what has heart and meaning for you personally which is, of course,
necessary in order that you can then align more meaningfully with
your organization and its varied stakeholders and be able to give of
your best when working to purpose and in role.

What the new paradigm also requires, however, is that you don't stop
there with the sense that that is the only reality. Instead, from that
grounded and rooted place you begin to cultivate a spirit of inquiry
and curiosity about your context and what it is that you do not yet
know or have not yet noticed about your emerging future.

As Einstein said, 'We don't know what we don't know' but we do
need to be mindful of finding out about it, if we are to flourish in an
uncertain environment that is increasingly emerging and co-created.
Otherwise the risk is that things going on in our world, that we had
not noticed, will catch up on us and knock us off track. Or simply,
that we will have missed out on helpful signs that were there for the
taking, about what was emerging for the future.

Kodak, for example, having invented digital technology nevertheless
missed out on the newly emerging market. It had not seen the signs
and instead stayed with its older, heretofore, reliable technologies.
The result was bankruptcy. Sony too. It had come up with the design
for the iPod before Apple, but again failed to notice the shifting market place and respond. I will look at these cases in greater detail in
Chapter 8. For the moment, however, the point to remember is that
in a context where the future is uncertain and emerging, one cannot
afford to not pay attention to the signs.

EXERCISE 5.7 A beginner's mind

The key way to develop openness is to develop what Suzuki (1970) terms a 'beginner's mind'. This means ceasing in being preoccupied with future worries, past regrets, and the infinite pictures that we tend to project onto any situation based on our previous experience. Instead, we try to develop the capacity to experience fully and freshly the uniqueness of every situation. The practice can take many different forms, but largely consists of spending some reflective time daily, if possible, and even if only for 10 minutes. During this time, what matters is that you consciously place your awareness onto something specific, be that your breath, your body, external sounds, the trees if you are out walking the dog, the food if you are eating or a simple external object, such as a candle. The object of focus is not what matters here, but the practice of remaining focused. Your mind will undoubtedly start wandering, moving you out of the present and back into threats and drives. This is perfectly normal and fine. You just have to then, kindly and gently, keep bringing your awareness back to the object of focus.

In terms of a practice, my rule of thumb is to pick something that you can enjoy. So, for example, often for me I will focus on external sounds if I am sitting, allowing them to come to me, or trees if I am out walking with the dog. That is easier for me than sitting with my breath, which is, however, one of the recommended ways to practice. You will need to find your own effective way in and different things will work better on different days, so having a range of practices is also very useful.

All manner of knowledge and insight will reveal themselves during this time. What is important is that you notice and observe these with curiosity, with a spirit of inquiry rather than judgement. And, that you are willing to be with whatever arises for you, allowing it to just be as it is; to simply accept it. The Dalai Lama, who apparently meditates for an hour each morning, was asked what he does when he has a very busy day. His reply was that he gets up an hour earlier and practises for two hours. Not, I hope you will appreciate, in order to space out but in order that he can then be so much more fully present and accountable throughout the remainder of that very busy day; so that he has the insights and resources that he needs to be able to meet the challenges that will arise and can therefore, working to his purpose, be more effective in his dealings with people. For him, being busy is not an excuse for mindless ineffectiveness.

EXERCISE 5.8 The three systems

Find a large piece of paper and draw three circles to scale to reflect the drive, threat and soothing systems outlined in Chapter 4 (three circles are easier for the purposes of this exercise than just one, as in Figure 5.5 opposite, but the principle is the same). So, if most of your time is spent worrying and ruminating in the threat system, then draw a big circle for it, while if you spend very little time feeling safe and content then draw a small circle for the soothing system. Once you have done this you can move on to the next part of the exercise.

Let's begin with the threat system. Think about the things that in your daily life right now trigger your threat system. It may be small things like getting to work on time, or your technology working or completing a piece of work; or it might be more serious things such as facing a divorce or a worrying health problem. Write these things in your threat circle. Think about how much of your time is spent in this emotional system and how often these concerns or worries pass through you.

Now pause and think about the things in life that give you pleasure and enjoyment; things that you feel excited about and look forward to; positive things that make you want to get out of bed each day. This could be something that you want to achieve or it might be the thought of going on holiday. It might be looking forward to a nice meal or a date with your partner. The key thing is the experience of being energized by whatever it is you think of. Write these in your drive circle. How preoccupied are you by things that excite you? How much time do you spend in this circle?

Now pause and think about the things in your life that give you a sense of slowing down, chilling out, being content and feeling a sense of well-being; not wanting to achieve anything or go anywhere because you are content with the way things are right now. What things, activities or relationships in your life foster this sense of feeling safe, connected and content? Write these in your soothing circle and then consider how much time you spend in the soothing system.

When you have completed all three circles, sit back and consider where you spend most of your time. It is not unusual for people to realize that it is the threat or drive system.

This exercise is reproduced with the kind permission of Choden.

FIGURE 5.5 The three systems

This Step 3, openness, asks you, therefore, to look again, beyond purpose and your known strengths, beyond your known knowns to any unknown knowns that might be emerging. This links to the idea presented in Chapter 4 of using your unconscious as a resource to help you see things that might not otherwise be apparent. Accessing that still quiet place, in order to find clues and signs, takes discipline and practice. Like trying to get physically fit, to do it well you will need to develop an attitude metaphorically that is the equivalent of spending time in the gym. However, if you do develop this discipline and practice on a regular basis, cultivating your present moment awareness in this way, then you will also be much more able to access this ability, as and when the going gets tough.

Exercises 5.7 and 5.8 above are designed to move you out of the threat and drive systems, described in Chapter 4, and into the soothing or parasympathetic system. The reason being that from here you will be able to cultivate spaciousness and stillness and increase your ability to see and notice things that you had not seen or noticed before. From this place, of being rather than doing, things will open up and reveal themselves to you in a way that they could not have done before. It is this knowing and discernment that will be required, more and more, from you as a leader or manager in your part of the business and what we will take forward into the next stage, wisdom and Step 4 of the Grounding Steps framework.

EXERCISE 5.9   Artist's date

Spend a block of time, perhaps two hours weekly, especially set aside
and committed to nurturing your creative consciousness, your inner artist. This
could be a walk in the park or a trip to a movie, a gallery, the theatre or a concert.
It can be anything that will give you pleasure. Do not take anyone with you.

This is a variant on the Three Systems exercise and one that I came
across in a book by Julia Cameron, *The Artist's Way* (1992). It was
a revelation to me, at that time, how little time I spent nourishing
myself. Instead, I seemed to be always doing or in the company of
others and it almost seemed inexcusable to have time off 'indulging'
myself in this way. That, in itself, was a significant learning and, of
course, the exercise makes perfect sense, for how can you possibly
notice things that might be emerging or, otherwise intangible, if you
are all the time busy on a treadmill? Nor is there ever any space left
for inquiry or new ideas. You could even ask what the point of life is
if not to have some personal pleasure.

EXERCISE 5.10   My now

Focus your attention on the steps outlined in Exercise 3.1 on page 44.

EXERCISE 5.11   Morning pages

Every morning write three pages in long-hand, strictly stream of
consciousness, with no right or wrong and strictly non-negotiable.

Again, this is a variation of Exercise 5.10 above and one that also comes from Julia Cameron's book, *The Artist's Way* (1992). The effect of doing this, in practice, is that you begin to become aware of the petty anxieties and fears that fill your being, the moods that hold you in their grip and the self-defeating critic that stops you in your tracks.

All of the exercises outlined within this Step 3, openness, will, with continued and regular practice, help you to connect to an inner power source that you did not know existed and from there, as if by magic, transform your understanding of your outer context and world. Surely a powerful tool for any business leader or manager today?

Step 4: Wisdom

> Until one is committed, there is hesitancy, the chance to draw back, always ineffectiveness. Concerning all acts of initiative and creation, there is one elementary truth the ignorance of which kills countless ideas and splendid plans: that the moment one definitely commits oneself, then providence moves too. All sorts of things occur to help one that would never otherwise have occurred. A whole stream of events issues from the decision, raising in one's favour all manner of unforeseen incidents, meetings and material assistance which no man could have dreamed would have come his way. Whatever you can do or dream you can, begin it. Boldness has genius, power and magic in it. Begin it now. (Johann Wolfgang von Goethe)

I mentioned, in the last section on openness, that increasingly what will be required from you, as a leader or manager within your business, is a more sophisticated level of knowingness and discernment concerning what steps you and your organization need to take in order to succeed. The Grounding Steps framework is designed to help you get to that place. First, by connecting with purpose, intention and motivation; second by developing insight and awareness into your unique strengths and gifts and therefore what you might also need to let go of; third, by cultivating a spirit of openness and inquiry about yourself and your organization within the wider context so that you can then begin to exercise wisdom and discernment in facing the choices and challenges ahead. The exercises now, for this Step 4 on wisdom, will take you further and into action from that place (see Figures 5.6, 5.7 and 5.8).

FIGURE 5.6 The Grounding Steps framework – expanded

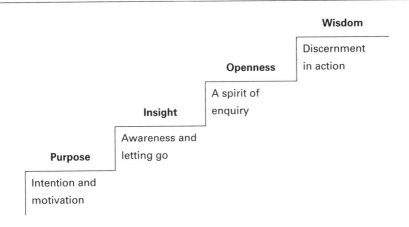

EXERCISE 5.12 Magic wand

Imagine you have a magic wand and that you can do almost anything with this wand. 'Wave' five things that you would like to have achieved in three years' time. Suspend judgement or evaluation at this stage and just make them up. What do they look like and feel like? Then assess and choose what specifically you would like to realize and write a detailed description of your ideal outcome. Then test it. Is it detailed enough? Does it need dates? What's missing?

A variation of this can also be done for something more specific like a changed role.

- Wave a magic wand and describe in detail the ideal job/role that you would like to be working at in three years' time.
- What skills are you using?
- What information are you working with?
- Where are you working, the location of travel?
- Who are your colleagues?
- Who are your clients?
- How much do you earn?

EXERCISE 5.13   Covey pie chart

Map onto a pie chart (A) your current distribution of activities. What percentage of time are you spending on each? Map onto a pie chart (B) your desired distribution of activities. What percentage of time would you like to spend on each? Name one thing that you could start/stop doing that would help you to get from (A) to (B).

EXERCISE 5.14   Three-year backwards

- Take a situation that you would like to change or create within your role.

- Identify the situation as it currently stands.

- Visualize how you would like the situation to appear in the future (three days, months, years).

- Imagine that you have already achieved your objectives, and draw a timeline back to today.

- Identify the specific actions that you took (past tense) in order to achieve your end result. Work backwards as it opens up more possibilities than working forwards (see Figure 5.7).

- Finally, convert your backward plan into a forward plan.

FIGURE 5.7   Three-year backwards

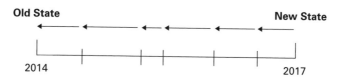

Three-year backwards, when completed, highlights the urgency of starting today if you really want to get to your desired state. Working backwards also frees up more possibilities and approaches than working forwards ever will, because you are working from your desired future and without fear, because you know that you have already arrived there. I have always found it quite amazing that this tool is used as a standard business planning model for banks when deciding whether to lend money. It is as if the bank is asking the organization to make up a story for them from an ideal future. That's the creative side of banking that I absolutely love.

EXERCISE 5.15 Force field analysis

This is an alternative way of approaching a similar situation.

- Take a situation that you would like to change or create within your role.

- Identify the situation as it currently stands.

- Visualize how you would like the situation to appear in the future (three days, months, years).

- Identify the existing forces operating in the current 'force field'. Drawing a line down the middle of a page, identify the driving forces on the left of the line and the restraining forces on the right (see Figure 5.8).

- Examine the forces. Which are strong, weak, and capable of influence, under your control?

- To develop a strategy in order to move the equilibrium from the current condition to the desired condition, do the following: add more driving forces; remove restraining forces; or do both.

- Implement the action plans. This should realize the desired condition.

This is a very practical model by Kurt Lewin (1940s) who understood that the forces and dynamics in the world of engineering and physics could also be applied within a social context. The power of the model is that it breaks any issue down into its various parts and enables one to see where the most effective action could be taken.

FIGURE 5.8 Force field analysis

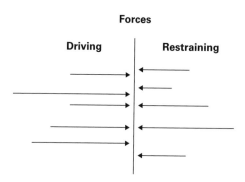

To conclude, a summary of all the exercises outlined above, and for each of the respective four steps of the Grounding Steps framework, is detailed in Figure 5.9.

FIGURE 5.9 The Grounding Steps framework – self

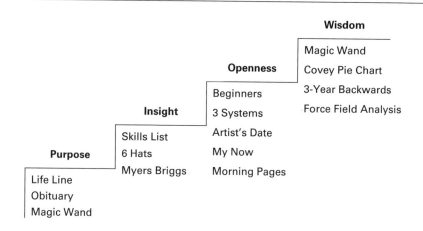

You hold the keys

You are one of the essential building blocks for your business. If you are to lead and manage effectively then, as I mentioned in Chapter 3, you will need to possess skills, such as EQ and a capacity for self-reflection, as well as being able to contain your anxiety in the face of complexity and change.

What will help greatly is, if in applying the Grounding Steps framework, you can:

- take responsibility for developing a really strong sense of who you are and what your overall purpose is in life;
- have a clear view of what you want from your future and can work backwards from that future;
- understand how to play into your natural strengths;
- know and accept your weaknesses;
- cultivate a spirit of inquiry and openness about the challenges and opportunities that present in life and work;
- tolerate not knowing, negative capability and in the words of Keats (1817) are 'capable of being in uncertainties, mysteries and doubts';
- take time for reflection and real discernment so that you can always be on the alert and listening for what might be being called forth from the business context at any given point in time; and
- working from the outside in being discerning about the steps required for you and your organization to flourish within a co-created emerging future.

The path that I recommend towards the enlightened organization is the two-pronged approach, which includes the personal as well as the systemic (see Figure 0.1 on page 3). You hold the keys to the success of the first prong, the personal, by knowing yourself more deeply through the exercises outlined in this chapter. You need, however, also to look more closely at the interpersonal, as we do in Chapters 6 and 7. In these chapters, the focus will be on how you interact with others in the performance of the task, including groups. Later, we will move the focus to the second prong, to system and context, which will be covered in Parts 3 and 4.

KEY POINTS

1 Self-awareness is key to being able to respond effectively as a leader or manager for the future.

2 The tools, techniques and framework outlined in this chapter can help you greatly to develop this capacity and skill.

3 The Grounding Steps framework will root you within your purpose and core strengths while also enabling you to remain open, flexible, discerning and able to act.

4 The various exercises contained within this chapter are designed to develop your connection with purpose, increase your level of awareness about the skills and strengths that you offer, generate a capacity for openness and a spirit of inquiry and ultimately enable you to be more discerning, when taking action in role and on behalf of your organization.

Ways into the other
Me and you

06

> *I want you to be all you can be, because that is the only way that I can be all I can be. I need you. I need you to be you, so that I can be me.* DESMOND TUTU

Two individuals working together form the next essential building block for any organization and this chapter focuses on the power that they have, when collaborating, to add real value and transform any business. This is crucial in the future reality where a flat networked organization seeks to sell its products or services globally by winning hearts and minds and retaining brand and reputation. The Roads to Resilience research, referred to in Chapter 3, found that:

> What links the Roads to Ruin and this new research is the central role executives play in building and sustaining strong and productive relationships, based on mutual trust, respect and inclusion, with customers, employees, shareholder, investors and other key stakeholders, which over time develop into loyalty and contribute to resilience. (Executive Summary, 2013)

However, we also saw in Chapter 4, that we can behave defensively towards others, if we feel that our needs are not being met by them or are otherwise threatened by what they represent. We can waste a tremendous amount of energy trying to defend ourselves against perceived threats from them and become very unproductive in the process.

This chapter looks at how we can combine our mutual and potentially unlimited resources to build something greater within the business than the sum of our individual and separate parts. It also demonstrates how we can only do this if we have first:

- understood why we react personally to others, in the way that we sometimes do;
- considered more fully who the other might really be beneath their exterior selves; and
- gained inner confidence in our own and their unique and authentic value and contribution to the business.

A short recap on theory

In Chapter 4, we looked at how two things can happen to us in our relationship with the other. First, having been shaped by our first experience of family and relationships we will have developed a 'known template' of our self, of the other and of the world; a fixed pattern of relating that worked for us back then and strategies for how to try to have our needs met in the world and therefore how best, we think, to relate, respond or react to the other. Second, we can often falsely imagine ourselves to be separate and potentially threatened by this unknown other and then do everything we can to avoid experiencing pain or anxiety from them. We will have developed unconscious defences that are designed to safeguard our self from any more harm in terms of, say, rejection or frustration, whatever are our primary fears. This is because these responses, if experienced from the other in the present, in the here and now, might trigger the enormous pain that we had first experienced earlier in our life (or evolving as humankind) when as a child we were rejected or frustrated. Defences are, therefore, designed to have us avoid dealing with the raw, sensitive, immature and underdeveloped or less evolved aspects of ourselves.

Defences against anxiety are therefore defences against the reality of what is actually taking place in the here and now between the two of us. So that when the other seemingly presents a stress too painful to bear, we regress to a form of primitive psychic defence mechanism and in doing so hope to avoid painful and vulnerable feelings such as anxiety, shame or guilt.

What are these defences? Well, there are many and we will explore them more fully in this chapter and in Chapter 7 when looking at groups. Meanwhile, however, let's recap on some of the major contenders that were outlined in Chapter 4. First, repression and denial. These are where you maintain an illusion that this is 'just not happening'. Second, splitting, where you experience your relationship with the other in terms of the infantile dichotomies of good and bad, failing to appreciate and therefore benefit from the richness and complexity that the other actually brings. Finally, projection and introjection. The former is where you attribute characteristics or feelings to the other that are in fact your own. The latter, where you assume feelings or characteristics that others project or the other projects onto you.

It is not personal

You can see that things between the two of you can, potentially, get very complicated and unreal. It is not personal, and neither one of you are to blame. It is simply part of the nature of being human. However, it is a tremendous waste of your combined resources and a great loss to the organization.

It will help enormously if you recognize this, and instead choose to both align on the overall purpose of the working relationship and what it is that unites you in terms of the business. It can also help greatly if you each stay clear and in touch with your separate strengths and weaknesses, as well as your individual roles and responsibilities. For, while some of your interactions with the other may seem personal, and may even be painful because of what they trigger in either one of you, the fact is that the relationship is not personal. It is a business relationship, where you each have your own separate roles and tasks that need to be performed and you're coming together to collaborate in order to better fulfil those tasks.

There are now two icebergs, yours and theirs, with superficial surface behaviour at the top, above the water line, and a depth of feelings, values, meanings and identities below, together with the unconscious (see Figure 4.3). It is important for you both to uncover more of what lies below the water line. Not because you need to get personal but because much of what you each have to offer lies dormant there, and the energy invested in keeping a lid on it all is wasted. If your energies are going in to maintaining defensive patterns of response, not only are you not building a closer relationship with the other but you are wasting the opportunity for realizing untapped potential and resources. Resources that are needed and essential to the business and the world we live in, if we are going to be able to address challenging times ahead.

The Grounding Steps framework

The exercises set out below, within the Grounding Steps framework, are designed to help you uncover the wealth of resources that exist between you – creative contributions to the organization that could not have been realized had you both been working separately nor without the alchemy of the unique relationship between you. The exercises will also help you to become more fully real with one another; to be able to be with what is actually occurring between you and to name what needs to be named, as the relationship progresses. This requires strength of character as well as a real commitment to the working purpose of your relationship. It also requires a great deal of self-awareness and insight, a genuine openness and curiosity about the other, and real wisdom and discernment in terms of your combined actions.

Step 1: Purpose

As we saw in Chapter 5, people get involved with organizations for all sorts of reasons. Money, security, relationships, a sense of value and belonging, self-esteem, recognition and in order to fulfil one's vocation or potential in life. Do you know why your other is involved with this organization and you? Other than money (if they get that), what do you think they get for themselves from working and being involved?

In an ideal world, theirs and your purpose will be closely aligned and certainly compatible. But to be able to say that requires that you first know what it is. That's a big question to ask of another, never mind, as we saw in the last chapter, our self. The exercises below will help you to understand more about what has heart, value and meaning for them. There are many ways in which more light can be shed and, depending on the closeness of the relationship between you, you can choose which of the exercises to use in practice.

EXERCISE 6.1 Magic wand

Imagine that both you and the other each have magic wands and can do almost anything with this wand. Then 'wave' five things that you would each like to have achieved at work by (some future date). Suspend judgement or evaluation at this stage and just make them up. What do they look like and feel like? Share and discuss this with each other. Then assess and choose what specifically you would each like to realize and write a detailed description of your ideal outcome that you can later share.

EXERCISE 6.2 Subjectives and objectives

Take a sheet of paper and draw a line down the middle. On the left hand side, write the heading 'Objectives' and within this column write down the objectives that you share over a given period, such as 6 or 12 months, in terms of progressing the business. For example, by September to have increased turnover by X%, increased profits by Y% or taken on five new clients.

When this column is completed, move to the other side of the page and mark a heading 'Subjectives'. In this column, note what you would each feel if you had achieved those objectives. What would you each get from that success? What are your unique subjectives? (See Figure 6.1 overleaf.)

EXERCISE 6.3 Values

Taking the key values of your organization, rank them in your own preferred order and then explain to each other what they mean for you personally and why you have ranked them in this way. Then, taking your top two or three explain how these have influenced you in your work and identify a time when one or more were actually challenged at work or were in conflict.

Then ask:

- What did you feel about what happened?

- Now, looking back, would you do anything differently?

- How might the outcome have changed if you had done things differently?

- Is there anything that you could do now to correct things for yourself or others?

FIGURE 6.1 Subjectives and objectives

Objectives	Subjectives
Turnover increased by X%	Proud Pleased New Skills
Profits increased by Y%	Excited Secure
	Confident Motivated
5 new clients	Sense of Achievement

Any or all of the three exercises above will help you to understand more about what has heart, value and meaning for your other. They will enable you both to connect more deeply with what has purpose and meaning for you in the work that you do, within your respective roles and on behalf of the organization. If you wanted to go further, say within a closer working relationship, you might also choose to share your respective life lines or obituaries, as described in Chapter 5. However, these would otherwise be inappropriate and should never be required of another.

Step 2: Insight

In this, step 2, you can begin to develop more understanding and appreciation of the talents and strengths that the other might be able to provide, so that you can then build on your combined potential within the business. There are simple ways of looking at this; for example, with De Bono's Six Thinking Hats, where this time your focus is on the other. Look at Figure 4.1 on page 55 and consider questions such as: Which two colours does your other prefer to use most of the time? Which are their least favourite colours? Through which colours do you engage with one another? And what might be missing?

Or you might like to try some more complex models, such as Myers Briggs, which we looked at in Chapter 5. Either way, I would also like to repeat the point made in that chapter that some of the exercises in this book can look deceptively easy while others can look deceptively hard. Please don't be fooled by appearances and try them out instead.

Myers Briggs and personality

We looked at this model in the last chapter and described its four polarities and broad temperaments in relation to self. In this chapter the focus is on the other and what we might share in common, or alternatively, provide by way of difference. We are going to use the model now to see if we can work out where the other would be on each of the four polarities. This is, of course, not an exact science as we are only guessing what we think. However, you could, of course, take this further and find a qualified practitioner to administer the test with both of you and then facilitate a session on the gifts you each offer, the pattern of relationship between you, areas of understanding as well as misunderstanding and why you might be relating to one another in a particular way. This is beyond the level of the book but let's see how far you can get by doing Exercise 6.4.

EXERCISE 6.4 Myers Briggs

This exercise can be done alone or together. Either way it can be useful to share your answers with one another.

- Mark where you think you and your significant other might be on each of the four polarities described in Figure 5.3 (on page 85).

- Which of the four temperaments described in Figure 5.4 (on page 86) do you think describes each of you the most?

- What might this mean for each of you within your respective roles?

- How might it affect your relationship with one another?

When we are working with the other, these personality differences can lead to misunderstandings and the widest gulf can often be between the sensing and intuitive types because they each experience the world so completely differently: the sensing person insisting on logic and facts and the intuitive person pushing proposals based on intuition and subjective experience. I find that the sensing person will naturally be drawn to a mechanical model such as force field analysis (see Figure 5.8 on page 97), whereas the intuitive person, preferring the future, will be drawn to three-year backwards (see Figure 5.7 on page 95). Of course, the end result will be the same, hence the power of the models and of providing alternative ways in, as different and more naturally suited ways of working.

Having the same personality type can lead to greater understanding but it can also give rise to difficulties in terms of competition and being more one-dimensional and ineffective. And, of course, it is also the very differences between us that can make for the most enormous contributions as well as affecting our ability to really co-create something different and meaningful between us. The challenge, therefore, is for us to really embrace this diversity through inclusion as the new organizational reality must. We do this, in practice, by understanding and appreciating the differences that others provide, so that we can together be aware of both our combined and separate strengths and weaknesses in relation to the tasks to be performed and the overall purpose of the business. That way we can each know how to work with and support the other to be our very best, thereby unleashing our combined untapped resources with authenticity and ease.

A simpler exercise, and one that works well when people are already aware of their strengths and weaknesses, is set out in Exercise 6.5 below.

EXERCISE 6.5 Help

- Share with each other the key skills, gifts and qualities that you think you can offer or provide.

- Say what it is that the other should know about you in order to get the best from you when working in role.

- Suggest ways in which you might collaborate and be more supportive of one another.

Step 3: Openness

One of things that happens when we develop a known template about self, the other and the world in general is that we then often behave as if this is real; the truth; the right and only way; particularly if we feel threatened or stressed at work. We lose any spaciousness and curiosity about others and find ourselves instead being critical, thinking that they have got it all wrong. But what if they were right? We often stop meaningfully enquiring about their perhaps different perspective and then lose out on this additional and potentially rich resource. In seeking premature closure, we carry on in our limited way with our 'known' template and are confirmed in our view that things are as we had worked out before, albeit in childhood. It is essential if we are to work well within the new paradigm that we learn to let go of this type of control and work instead to cultivate a spirit of openness and inquiry about others. They are a huge potential resource to us and we need to not push them away in this fashion or try to mould them to our own likeness. If we do, the risk is that nothing new can emerge or be co-created between us.

Conversations are the new work

The poet David Whyte said, 'Conversations are not about the work, they are the work', and this is certainly true in the context of building openness in our relationship with the other. It is in the dialogue between two people that the chemistry can build, the alchemy take place, and new ideas and resources emerge.

Thomas Moore, a famous Irish poet, said: 'To have real conversations with people may seem like such a simple obvious solution but it involves courage and risk.' Why so? The majority of my clients will admit to having a conversation that needs to be had but which they would prefer to avoid. And when I enquire as to why, 100 times out of 100, they will admit to being afraid of the response from the other. This brings us back to Freud and the pleasure/pain principle. People would prefer to avoid the conversation, regardless of the cost in the longer term, because of the possible feelings that it might evoke.

Some fear fight as a response from the other, which might look like attack, anger, rage or blame. Others fear flight, which might look like withdrawal, upset or denial. Others are more afraid of the feelings that the conversation might evoke within themselves, such as shame, rejection or getting it wrong/not being perfect. Ultimately, at its core there is a fear that the other's response might trigger some earlier pain from childhood and maybe even lead to a loss of status or role within the organization – a form of death in the business context. So, people do have very real fears.

However, as has been mentioned earlier, the good stuff in terms of what has heart and meaning, what has value, and any greater potential or creativity that might be created between two people is also all below the water line. The dilemma is that you can't really get there without going through feelings (see Figure 4.3 on page 57). You have to dig down if you are to get to what matters to you both and if you are to be capable of combining your unlimited resourcefulness: digging for gold. Instead, by avoiding the conversation you are, at best, wasting energy keeping a lid on matters, and, at worst, colluding in behaviours that are not in line with purpose and could possibly harm the organization. We can look again at the Roads to Ruin case studies and wonder how many of billions of conversations were not had back then and that are still not being had?

In Chapter 3 we looked at the competencies and skills that are required for leaders and managers for the future. These included EQ, as well as competence in terms of stakeholder communications. In particular, the ability to:

- develop the conversational life of the organization in order to make creativity possible;
- be constantly vigilant for unconscious group processes that might be trapping conversations in repetitive themes;
- contain the anxiety of complexity and change for others;
- build trust between all stakeholders and especially those engaged in difficult conversations;
- embrace and integrate diversity; and
- engage hearts and minds, enabling strategies and the future to emerge.

It follows that it will be important for you, as a leader or manager within the organization, to overcome any personal fears and begin to engage in the conversational nature of your relationships within the context of the overall purpose of the business. If you are truly working to purpose then it is your right as well as your responsibility to do so.

In that respect, a theory or framework can always be helpful. Kurt Lewin coined the phrase that 'there is nothing as practical as a good theory'. I use three particular frameworks that clients say really help them to develop openness in their conversations with others. The first, 'Johari Window', describes the way in which you choose to communicate with others and how open or closed you are with them. The second, 'Courageous Conversations', is designed for the more difficult conversation, where maybe something has been building up between you both or there is, otherwise, some form of misunderstanding between you. The third, called 'Daily Temperature Reading', is designed to oil the wheels of a close relationship on an ongoing basis and is as relevant in the good times as it is in the bad.

Johari Window

Openness can be illustrated by means of a diagram called the 'Johari Window' (so called because it was developed by two psychologists Joe Luft and Harry Ingram (1955)). See Figure 6.2 below.

FIGURE 6.2 Johari Window

	Known to Self	Unknown to Self
Known to Others	**OPEN**	**BLIND**
Unknown to Others	**HIDDEN**	**UNKNOWN**

The model in theory

The 'window' describes three categories of behaviour: 'open', 'blind' and 'hidden'. Behaviour that can be described as 'open' is perceived and known by both you and the other. As your relationship deepens, the open pane gets bigger, reflecting your willingness to be known. It will include things you know and don't mind admitting about yourself.

'Blind' behaviour describes actions and manners of behaviour that have an effect on the other but of which you are unaware. Others may, for example, see you as abrasive and controlling while you see yourself as kind and easy-going. Or you may think of yourself as confident and self-assured but because of nervous mannerisms others may see your insecurities. The more that you learn about the qualities in your blind pane the better you will be able to relate to others, because it will put you in touch with their reality. I will look at how you can do this in practice below.

'Hidden' behaviour refers to facts, emotions and feelings that you are aware of but that you deliberately choose not to share with the other. This can be a perfectly legitimate thing to do as there will undoubtedly be many issues that you could reveal but that are not related to the overall purpose or your role. Provided you are consciously making that choice then it is right to keep them here.

The shaded area, referred to as the 'Unknown' pane, is really what Freud and others referred to as our unconscious, being made up of everything that is unknown to you and the other. This includes all your untapped resources, all your potential and everything about you that currently lies dormant.

The model applied

The panes will be different for every 'other' that you relate to and they too will have their own panes in relation to you. The configuration of the size of the panes will also change with each individual relationship over time, with close colleagues enjoying more of an open pane, as the relationship between the two of you deepens and evolves. The interdependence of the panes means that a change in the size of one of the panes will affect all others. For example, let's say the other tells us that we seemed to be nervous when we had actually felt confident and assured, this of itself would enlarge the open pane between us.

The question to ask yourself in every relationship is: Do I want to increase the size of my open pane in relation to this person? Would doing so be working to purpose and in service to my role? Because, of course, if it is not, then arguably why would you? Let's assume that in a case of a certain hypothetical other you have decided that it would be good to have a deeper, more intimate understanding of one another. How could you do this in practice? Well, in a number of ways.

First you might choose to reveal more about yourself and by bringing more of yourself to the relationship you increase the size of the open pane and automatically reduce the size of the others. Often people spend an enormous amount of energy trying to avoid becoming known by the other. Why – what might they be afraid of? Rejection, failure to get support, hurting the other or fear maybe that they are not interested in what they have to say?

Another way in which you might increase the size of the open pane is to invite feedback from the other about your blind pane. It can be rewarding and satisfying to gain insight in this way, but it can also be painful when we hear things that we would have preferred not to have heard. It is for that reason that the blind pane is also referred to as the 'Garlic breath' corner. However, the more truth that you are willing to accept from others, the more accurate your self-concept will be and the smaller this box will remain over time.

EXERCISE 6.6 Johari Window

- Take some key stakeholders that represent significant others for you in your role.

- Examine each of them in terms of the Johari Window. What size are the panes?

- Are there things that you could reveal but are not prepared to do so? Why so? Are you afraid of their reaction if you do?

- Have you received feedback from this other about your blind pane? In which case, did you agree with the feedback?

- Are there things that have been hidden that might better be off being revealed? Or things revealed that might have been better hidden?

- What, if anything, are you learning about yourself through this relationship?

Courageous conversations

This model has three parts: your opening, followed by the opportunity to really listen to the other and then finally a dialogue between the two of you. The part that we will look at here is what I call your 'opening statement' because if you can prepare for that, paying attention to what it is you really want to say, then you can really relax and listen well to the other. You will then be safely anchored by what you have already prepared for and said, and therefore better able to respond to what the other might bring to light. Your opening statement includes six elements, each made up of one or two lines only and the whole thing should take no longer than a couple of minutes to speak. That is why the preparation is so crucial because otherwise you will lose your audience (see Figure 6.3).

First, you need to say what it is you want to talk about. I know that this seems altogether obvious, but very often people just launch into conversations without having thought through clearly what it is they specifically want to address, and leaving the other party fairly confused. This happens even more where there is nervousness or anxiety on either side of the conversation.

FIGURE 6.3 Six-step opening statement

Be Clear, Brief and Focused:

1. Topic or theme and example... *be specific*
2. My feelings... *ownership, vocabulary and congruence*
3. Why it matters... *business case/shorter term*
4. The implications... *business case/longer term*
5. Maybe I... *my part in this with honesty and humility*
6. What I'd like is... *for you and I... aim and purpose... open*

Second, address the feelings in the conversation instead of pretending that they are not there, hiding underneath the water line and waiting to come up and bite you. Say how you feel about the issue and having this conversation. Are you nervous, excited, upset or confused? Whatever it is, say it, as long as it is congruent with how you are actually feeling. If not, the other will notice and you will have lost your authenticity with them. Be real. Say how you feel. Not as blame; that the other made you feel this way, but just say it as it is. Why? Because it will stop those feelings from trying to sabotage the conversation later on and it will enable them to surface up to above the water line. This will help both of you to breathe and also give the other permission to acknowledge their own feelings. Try it out for yourself and see how it has the effect of altering the whole level at which you can now have the conversation from that point on. You are not asking them to fix you emotionally, nor you them, but you are saying that this is what is going on for you and that it is real and that it matters. Once said, paradoxically you will find that you have more energy and are freed up then to move on to the third step.

As I said earlier, the personal is not why you are both together having this conversation and all of this is only relevant if it in some way affects the business. The third step, therefore, is to say why this issue matters in terms of the business case in the shorter term. Here again, your preparation is key because it takes hard work to really think through the implications in a clear and helpful way that can then be heard by the other.

Fourth, consider the implications of not addressing the issue in the terms of the business case, longer term. It is important to really think this through because this affects the ultimate purpose of the business and is an area on which you should already be both fully united and aligned. Why does this matter to the business? Clarity and good reasoning are crucial here and it will not always be easy. If we think, for example, about some of the conversations that should have happened at senior levels in the Roads to Ruin case studies, one can see that presenting the worst-case scenarios of bankruptcy and collapse might have taken great vision and great courage. However, it needed to be done and it wasn't.

Fifth, we own up to our part in the matter: 'Maybe I have been too slow in speaking up or maybe I am being overly sensitive but…'. This helps to diffuse any reactive response from the other, because we are already being big enough to own our part in the place that we both now find ourselves in. It can also disarm them slightly, in the best possible way, so as to create a more collaborative approach to the conversation and one that is perceived as less adversarial. It also invites the other to admit fault, on their part, without being made to feel wrong.

Sixth, we ask for what we want. Again, not rocket science but it is amazing how many times I see people preferring to shirk a direct request like this, especially when they are nervous about the conversation. But why are you having it if there is not something that you want the two of you to address? Being clear is going to be much more helpful for the other than glossing over it.

An example

Let's look at an example so that you can see the six steps more clearly. Joe, a senior manager is at a team meeting where Jane, one of his colleagues, constantly interrupts him. This has the effect of silencing him in front of the others and he realizes, after the meeting, that there was something important that he needed to address with another team member Bill which, instead, got forgotten. He makes an appointment to speak with Jane about this and prepares his opening statement, which he delivers after all the appropriate niceties.

> I would like to talk to you about your style of communication at the meeting last week and, in particular, the manner in which I was interrupted by you.

I felt undermined and silenced.

It is important that we discuss this because it impacts on all of our performance. For example, there was something that I needed to bring up with Bill which was subsequently overlooked and maybe there were others at the meeting who felt the same.

Longer term this would not be good for team relations and hence our overall performance within the business.

Maybe I am being overly sensitive or petty.

But I would like to discuss this with you so that we can see how we might address it going forward.

Now you are free to hand over to the other and to really listen to how they perceive the issue. Neither of you are right or wrong. However, if you have prepared and can speak clearly, as outlined above, you will be in a much better position to be able to be fully present to hear what it is they have to say. When you have truly listened to the other, in this open way, then that is when you can begin to have a real dialogue between you and when new insights and understandings can arise.

Finally, remember that while you have the right and the responsibility to have this conversation you cannot shake hands with a clenched fist. You need the resources of the other in order to address the issue and thereby achieve the business purpose. You both need to work together on it. So go into the conversation with a positive intention towards them and a real belief in the enormity of what your shared resources can bring to the understanding and ability to address the issue.

EXERCISE 6.7 Opening statement

Think of a courageous conversation that you need to have with a significant other or a courageous conversation that you had or should have had in the past.

Prepare your six-step opening statement.

EXERCISE 6.8 Self-audit

Draw a line down the centre of a couple of pages and on the right hand side of the page write down your imagined dialogue with the other.

When you have finished this imaginary dialogue, you then move to the column on the left hand side and there you write everything that you are thinking and feeling about that dialogue.

- How many pages did each column run into?

- What have you learnt from the left-hand column about your known template of reality as well as your potential areas of reactivity?

- How might this now inform the way in which you might prepare for the conversation?

The left hand column can often run to five or ten times more than the right. Why? Because it unpacks an enormous amount of baggage that would otherwise have somehow leaked into your communication whether you had wanted it to or not. Instead, you can now use the insights there, information which was largely otherwise in your unknown pane, to inform you about what best to say and what best not to say or otherwise communicate in the dialogue. In other words, what to put in your open pane and what might be much better left in your hidden pane.

Daily temperature reading

The 'Daily Temperature Reading' was developed by Virginia Satir (1978) as a way of helping people in a close longer-term relationship to communicate in a clear and effective way. It can be especially helpful to use with close colleagues at work, and suggests keeping the following five areas current and alive between you:

- appreciations;
- new information;

- puzzles;
- complaints with recommendations; and
- wishes, hopes and dreams.

The model suggests that, at some regular interval, you sit down together and each of you goes through the five areas in sequence.

Appreciations

So I might start by saying what it is that I appreciate about you and you then take your turn to say what it is you appreciate about me. It helps to be specific so that you can build your understanding of what this means in terms of your day-to-day role within the business. So often we forget that there are lots of things that we like about the other, even if there is this one thing that they might have done to annoy us. Our mind is like Velcro – it lets the negative stick.

Appreciating what it is about the other that we like is a great way of acknowledging them and building our relationship while also reminding ourselves of what it is more specifically that they bring to the relationship that would otherwise be absent.

New information

So much of what can go wrong in a working relationship is that we are not given the information we need to fully understand what is going on for the other person, so there is too much room left for assumptions. Updating each other on our state, mood and generally what is going for us in work or life is a great way of keeping current and real together.

Puzzles

If there are things that you don't understand or are curious or puzzled about, this is the time to clear them up. This shows that you care and builds understanding and trust in each other.

Complaints with recommendations

This is a chance to say if something bothers you and might be eating away at the relationship but maybe is difficult to say. It should not be blaming or judgemental but instead clear because it is about you and your needs not theirs. It might go something like this:

'When you said that you would have that report for me on the 16th and then gave it to me three days later, I was irritated and upset. I would prefer it if you could let me know when you will actually deliver something to me, in real time, or advise me if there is going to be a delay. That way, I can organize my other work accordingly.'

So you need to specify the behaviour that you are complaining about and what you would prefer. There is no guarantee that the other person will accept your recommendation. This is more a question of being real and a first step in facing, airing and then maybe dealing with some of the potential pitfalls within your working relationship. It is also a way of revealing more about yourself and thereby building understanding and trust.

Wishes, hopes and dreams

You will appreciate by now that our wishes, hopes and dreams are integral and vital to who we are in life, in business and in relationships with others. It is a core part of who we are as people and therefore what we bring, as added value, to building the success of our organization. In sharing them with the other we expand our own possibilities and future and extend our sense of safety, excitement and goodwill towards the other. The more that we can both bring these into our mutual awareness and talk about them, the more possibility there is that they will be realized.

EXERCISE 6.9   The DTR

- Take a significant other that you like and work closely with or take, by way of practice, a friend or family member.

- Agree with one another that you will do the DTR together once a week for a minimum period of one month.

- See how you get on and then decide whether you would each like to continue and whether you might like to start the process with someone else.

Step 4: Wisdom

Wisdom is the fourth step within the Grounding Steps framework and involves, first, stopping to assimilate the information that has been gathered from the three earlier steps. This, so that you can then be more discerning about the actual steps that you and your other should now, from this new vantage point, be taking if working effectively to purpose and on behalf of your organization. The Grounding Steps framework is designed to help you both get to that place. First, by connecting you with each other's purpose, intention and motivation; second, by developing insight and awareness into your combined strengths and gifts and third, by cultivating a spirit of openness and inquiry about each other and the wider context so that you can both now begin to exercise wisdom and discernment in facing the choices and challenges that lie ahead.

From here you can plan out the path ahead together by using Exercises 5.12–5.15, Magic Wand, Covey Pie Chart, Three-Year Backwards and Force Field Analysis. See Figure 6.4 for a summary of all of the exercises that can be applied when working with the other during each of the four steps of the Grounding Steps framework.

Open the door

My approach to the enlightened organization is, as outlined before, a two-pronged approach: the personal and interpersonal in the first prong, and system and context in the second. You hold the keys to the personal by knowing yourself more deeply through the exercises outlined in Chapter 5. You now also hold some of the keys to the interpersonal, through discovering more about the other and the resources that can be co-created between you. These skills will be critical to your overall success within a flat networked business that is seeking to sell its products or services globally by winning hearts and minds and retaining brand and reputation.

Both you and the other have the capacity to achieve so much more together in terms of quality deliverables than either of you could by doing it alone. Only, however, if you are both aligned and working effectively to purpose. That takes commitment on both sides of the relationship but particularly yours. The organization cannot do any of this for you, although it must provide the support required. And

FIGURE 6.4 The Grounding Steps framework – other

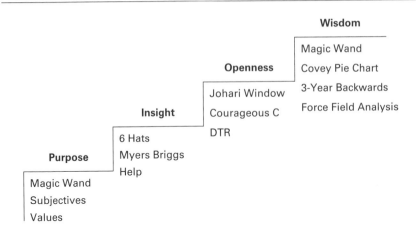

the other might be a critical stakeholder who works outside of the organization, and maybe has not yet read this book. So I am handing you the keys to open the door and start the process off. Change can only begin with one person taking a giant leap for mankind and the new organizational reality requires that you self-authorize in terms of what is needed for the business to succeed. So, once again in the words of David Whyte: 'Put down the weight of your aloneness and ease yourself into the conversation… with the other.'

KEY POINTS

1 Two people collaborating together can add real value and transform any organization.

2 They can, however, instead each feel threatened and behave defensively with one another, leading to a needless amount of inefficiency on both sides and a considerable wasted opportunity.

3 It is important to recognize that the relationship is not personal, even if it might at times feel that way, and to instead align with and work towards the overall purpose that unites you both and drives the organization.

4 Engaging skilfully in real and authentic conversations with a wide and diverse community of others is critical to the success of a networked organization that aspires to operate successfully within the new reality.

5 It will be in the dialogue between two people that alchemy can take place and new ideas and resources emerge.

6 The tools, techniques and frameworks outlined in this chapter can really help. First, by connecting you with each other's purpose, intention and motivation; second, by developing insight and awareness into your combined strengths and gifts and third, by cultivating a spirit of openness and curiosity about each other and the wider context so that you can both then begin to exercise wisdom and discernment in facing the choices and challenges that lie ahead.

Ways into the group
Me, you and others too

07

> *Never doubt that a small group of thoughtful committed citizens can change the world; indeed, it's the only thing that ever has.* MARGARET MEAD

You should never underestimate the potential power that can be realized from any of the groups you work in. The trick is being able to realize that power because groups can be messy places to work, with members playing all sorts of different roles and responding to a multitude of preferred and subjective ways of being in the world.

Group performance has been of interest to management writers for over 100 years, but is all too often seen in terms of individual performance multiplied by the group numbers. In reality, groups have a whole different life force of their own. And while the work that you will have done at an individual level, following Chapter 5, and with another, following Chapter 6, will be important groundwork, there is more that you need to understand about yourself and others in order to be able to work effectively in groups. Let's look at some of the theory.

Belbin and the perfect team

Meredith Belbin (1981) was fascinated by the question of what makes an 'ideal' team. Was it nature or nurture? He used teams of managers playing business games to identify the effects on group performance of different personality 'roles' and showed that some 'roles' work more effectively together while others do not and that 'role' has a greater impact on performance than the individual abilities of the people involved. He found that teams made up of people simply on the basis of their ability, no matter how clever they are, do not make for the better performing teams. Instead, teams designed to include a balance of different personality types or 'roles' are much more likely to win even if they do not contain the most able individuals; it is actual contribution and interdependence that determine performance.

According to Belbin, we each of us have our preferred ways of contributing to a team which are not necessarily exclusive preferences for one role or another and the strength of our preferences may vary. These patterns of behaviours or roles are described in Figure 7.1.

Belbin discovered nine essential roles for effective team performance. Regardless of the number of team members, all nine roles need to be played, so some people may have to play more than one role. According to his model, so long as people play to their strengths all will be well, as their inevitable weaknesses can be compensated for by others contributing these as their own strengths. Together then, as a balanced team, they can be successful.

Belbin's roles correlate well with other personality profiles such as Myers Briggs, mentioned in earlier chapters, so that if someone is, for example, an ENFP on Myers Briggs then they are likely to have a high preference for the 'Shaper' and 'Plant' Belbin roles; whereas an ISTJ on Myers Briggs is more likely to prefer the roles of 'Monitor Evaluator' and 'Completer Finisher'.

Belbin's model is a useful way of examining behaviours within a team and why they might be arising, of understanding people's individual strengths and weaknesses and of seeing how individuals can best support each other more effectively. It also highlights which roles might be missing and therefore need to be compensated for, if the team is to be a winning team.

Problematic teams might be made up of two or more dominant Shapers, none of whom is willing to give up 'shaping'; a Chair together with two dominant Shapers; no Resource Investigator in a team operating in a competitive environment; too many Plants but no Monitor Evaluators and Completer Finishers or too many Monitor Evaluators, Company Workers and Completer Finishers, but no Plants and

FIGURE 7.1 Belbin roles

Roles and Descriptions

	Team-Role Contribution		Allowable Weaknesses
	Plant	Creative, imaginative, unorthodox. Solves difficult problems.	Ignores incidentals. Too preoccupied with own thoughts to communicate effectively.
	Resource Investigator	Extrovert, enthusiastic, communicative. Explores opportunities. Develops contacts.	Over-optimistic. Can lose interest once initial enthusiasm has passed.
	Co-ordinator	Mature, confident. Clarifies goals. Brings other people together to promote team discussions.	Can be seen as manipulative. Offloads personal work.
	Shaper	Challenging, dynamic, thrives on pressure. Has the drive and courage to overcome obstacles.	Prone to provocation. Liable to offend others.
	Monitor Evaluator	Serious minded, strategic and discerning. Sees all options. Judges accurately.	Can lack drive and ability to inspire others.
	Teamworker	Co-operative, mild, perceptive and diplomatic. Listens, builds, averts friction.	Indecisive in crunch situations.
	Implementer	Disciplined, reliable, conservative in habits. A capacity for taking practical steps and actions.	Somewhat inflexible. Slow to respond to new possibilities.
	Completer Finisher	Painstaking, conscientious, anxious. Searches out errors and omissions. Delivers on time.	Inclined to worry unduly. Reluctant to let others into own job.
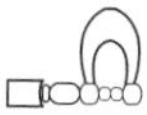	Specialist	Single-minded, self-starting, dedicated. Provides knowledge and skills in rare supply.	Contributes on only a limited front. Dwells on specialised personal interests.

Resource Investigators, the latter group being very efficient at doing the wrong thing.

And certainly some thought could also be given to the balance of roles within the new organizational paradigm and whether some have now become more valuable, such as Plant, in terms of change and needing new ideas about the context, and maybe Resource Investigator, in terms of building networks and more interconnectedness.

EXERCISE 7.1   Belbin roles

- Can you recognize some of the Belbin roles being played out in the groups that you work in?
- Which two of Belbin's team roles do you consider to be your stronger preferences when working in a group?
- Which two are your weaker ones?
- What are the implications of this for the groups that you work in?

Forming, storming, norming and performing

The other way into groups is to think about them more in terms of their evolution or development. Bruce Tuckman (1965) describes this in terms of four critical phases of development:

- **Forming** – where members are still polite, watchful, guarded and inhibited with one another. They are finding their feet in the group.
- **Storming** – where members begin challenging and questioning what they are doing, who they are being in relation to one another and why they are working together. For what purpose and why in this way? This stage can be challenging and painful, especially if progress is experienced to be slow.
- **Norming** – where members begin to develop skills in relation to the task, establish procedures and gather feedback. They are building their interpersonal relationships with one another and beginning to find routes by which to confront the challenges that they face as a team.
- **Performing** – where the team members have matured together and are now resourceful, flexible, open and supportive. At this stage they are at a sufficient level of efficiency that their energies can be directed for the benefit of the team.

FIGURE 7.2 The Grounding Steps framework – why, who, what, how?

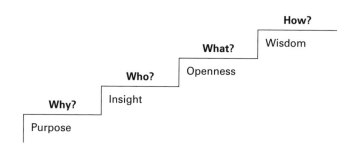

This is essentially the why, who, what and how of groups and in many ways maps neatly onto the Grounding Steps framework

The working group

One of the limitations of the Belbin model in terms of our current and future organizational structures is that we are each of us less likely to be operating within a stable team environment made up of the requisite nine roles. Instead, we increasingly find ourselves working within and across a diverse range of working groups, the constitution of which may be constantly changing, and with less and less opportunity for meeting face to face.

And while Tuckman's forming, storming, norming and performing model is insightful and helpful, the reality is that, in practice, people underestimate the task involved in truly addressing the questions about why and who, at the first two stages. This can be especially so when the pressure is on to deliver, as it so often is, and the leader or manager within the group then defaults to their solo performer's competency approach. This links to a point that I made earlier, in Chapter 3, about leaders and managers having been traditionally developed and rewarded for their individual competencies and skills as 'solo performers', without regard to their weaker shadow sides and, in particular, their level of competence in terms of collaborating with others and leading through these increasingly interconnected, complex and changing times.

Individual behaviour writ large

Wilfred Bion, one of the great group behavioural psychologists, said that 'Group behaviour is individual behaviour writ large' (1955).

What he meant by this was that all of the issues that we have looked at, in Chapters 5 and 6, apply equally within a group context – if not more so. Within a group you will find as many of Freud's icebergs as there are members of the group, and you will need to get below the surface behaviour and the water line of each one of them if you are to surface gold. To build relationship capability within the group you will need to be able to find out who the members are in relation to one another? What strengths they each bring? What weaknesses? What fires them up and makes their heart sing? What you each see as the genuine purpose of the group? You also need to become aware of the defensive patterns of response that can get in the way of the group's overall performance. We can use the Grounding Steps framework to explore these areas within a group, as we have done for self and other in the last two chapters.

The group as a whole

But that is not the whole picture. An understanding of individual differences and interpersonal relations in organizations, while very helpful, is not quite enough. As I said in Chapter 4, when looking at interconnectedness, the individual and the group will each be affecting and influencing one another. For example, a group may exert such a strong influence on its individual members that shared patterns of unconscious behaviours, such as splitting and projection, arise. Foulkes and Anthony (1965) refer to this group consciousness as the 'Matrix', which can in ways be thought of as a separate iceberg – the group's iceberg as an amalgam of the sum of the individual members. Certainly, we will all have had experiences of this: of being inspired and, in part, governed by the collective forces of a whole group. The skill for leaders and managers, and indeed all of us that work in groups, is to be able to work with that awareness.

The Grounding Steps framework

So how do you do this in practice? Well, in part, by going back to the Grounding Steps framework and the tools that I have described in earlier chapters and, in part, by becoming more aware of and working with the concept of the group as a whole and how it can also help or hinder performance. Loose networks and cross-functional working groups are becoming the new norm and their effectiveness largely dependent on the ability of the group to self-reflect in practice and for you and each of the members to take responsibility for their part in that process.

Step 1: Purpose

You must, at all costs, continuously explore and agree on the purpose of the group and why the task that you have set yourselves matters to the business, to this group and to each of the individual members. What is the intention behind this particular task and what is the motivation for group members? Once this is clarified you can then negotiate and renegotiate the different roles that each of you will play in order to best achieve your desired objectives and purpose.

Within the future reality none of this may be clear or a given at the outset. It may well be that a significant part of the work of the group is to align on purpose and to design, redesign and continuously self-authorize in role. No working group, whatever paradigm it is operating within, will be at its best if its members are unclear about their purpose or their role.

This is quite a considerable task and one that, without good leadership, can often get bypassed with groups rushing instead, prematurely, to the planning and doing phase before they have properly enquired into questions such as who is in the group and why they are a group. But the whole nature of the new paradigm built, as it is, on relationship, heart and values, interconnectedness and inclusiveness means that the answer to these questions is more critical than ever.

If anyone is uncertain or unclear then the whole group potentially falls short because it may be that it is this very person who finds themselves at their edge, in the context of a particularly important challenge, and having to make a strategic decision or communication based on the values and ethos of the company. If they are not fully aligned and self-authorized, they may well not be able to make the most appropriate judgement call. That's the risk then that the whole group takes. Take, by way of example, the situation described in Chapter 1, of the supermarket manager, in transit at an airport, having to respond to news about traces of horsemeat that were found in burgers that they sold. Having a deep understanding of who they are as a business and what they stand for will be crucial to how well he or she responds.

BP's Gulf of Mexico spill is an example of where a group member's response did not turn out well. Downplaying the incident, the CEO Tony Hayward (2010) called the amount of oil and dispersant 'relatively tiny' in comparison with the 'very big ocean'. Hayward also initially stated that the environmental impact of the Gulf spill was likely to be 'very, very modest'. Later, he said that the spill was a disruption to Gulf Coast residents and to himself, adding, 'You know, I'd like my life back.' Understandably, none of this went down very well. By contrast, the speed of Coca-Cola's decision (2003), made within 24 hours of the troubled UK launch of Dasani, indefinitely to abandon the launch, shows that the company knew how to protect its reputation and brand. Dasani, the troubled drink never did reappear on shelves.

There are many other examples in the Roads to Ruin research, referred to in Chapter 2, of where members of a working group have misunderstood or lost sight of the purpose and the core values on which they were meant to have been aligned. These proved, in some instances, to be catastrophic in terms of brand value and reputation not to mind, in some instances, also having a significantly negative impact on the wider community.

EXERCISE 7.2   Why?

Ask the following questions:

- What is the overall purpose of this group? Why do we exist? To what end? And in what ways might we add value to the business?

- What values, if any, do we hold dear?

- What is the intention behind this particular objective or task?

- How is it related to overall purpose?

- What is the motivation for each of us as members of this group? What will we get from having achieved the objectives?

Step 2: Insight

There are two elements to developing group insight. First, appreciating preferences and how better to understand and, therefore, utilize the talents and strengths of individual members within the team. You can use the techniques and models outlined in earlier chapters to explore preferences, strengths and weaknesses within the group as well as any gaps. These are listed in Figure 7.3 and would simply need to be adapted to a group context. You can then consider how best, in working to the purpose of the organization, to take up significant roles within the group.

Second, understanding and being able to work more effectively with the process of the group itself. This is where we can work with the blocks that might otherwise affect performance and impede the progress of the task. According to the psychological theories, we have each been shaped by our very first experience of groups, which was our first family. From there we have created a 'known' subjective and deficit template for how best we think, to relate, respond or react within groups. All of this might have worked reasonably well back then within our first family but may not be the most effective way of relating within this particular working group.

Individual members will each bring their own unique deficit templates into the working group and then, at times when feeling anxious or threatened, by the other members of the group or the nature of the task, resort to unconscious defences against their anxiety such as repression, denial, splitting, projection and introjection, which were described in Chapter 4, as well as maybe many more. It follows that we need to attend to the irrational or darker side of what lies below the water line as much as to the lighter elements. We need to attend to the patterns of behaviour that we assume unconsciously, when anxious or threatened, in an attempt to protect ourselves from painful feelings such as incompetence, vulnerability, guilt or rejection.

The challenge when working in groups is to be able to understand these patterns of reactivity and response and somehow be able to get the group out of the pit when they arise. Otherwise, they will take the energy of the individual members which should, more appropriately, be directed in the performance of the task. Let's look, first, at some of these defensive patterns of response before considering how we can best then get you of out of any pit.

Defences against anxiety

Repression, *Denial*, *Projection* and *Introjection*: Let me recap on these defences, as they were outlined in Chapter 4. First, repression and denial. These are where you maintain an illusion that this is 'just not happening'. Second, splitting, where you experience your relationships in terms of the infantile dichotomies of good and bad, failing to appreciate and therefore benefit from the richness and complexity that they actually bring. Finally, projection and introjection. The former is where you attribute characteristics or feelings to others that are in fact your own. The latter, where you assume feelings or characteristics that others project onto you.

Competition is where a member feels the need to win at all costs. They might speak first, shape the task, oppose others' views or have to be right. Competition flexibly used can be great as you might be the best person to lead. It becomes defensive when you are always competing.

Narcissism is all about 'me me me'. These members might take centre stage, continuously wanting the limelight all of the time, use the other members as their audience, demand approval and applause, like the sound of their own voice and not rate other contributions as being as valuable as their own.

Pleasing is where the member is continually deferent to some or all of the other members. They may be exceedingly helpful, organizing the practicalities for everyone and overly compliant. They will ask for permission for things, not take risks and be more focused on harmony within the group relationships than they are on the performance of the task. This defence mechanism is about seeking approval from the group at the expense of authentic self-expression.

Collusion is where some or all members become forcefully united with one another regardless of the task. They might back up other members who have the same agenda, give the narcissist the air time or encourage the pleaser and certainly they will join in with some of the denials, splits and projections or introjections operating within the group.

Pairing is being close to another specific member of the group to the exclusion of other members. The pair might always sit beside each other, exchange knowing looks, address their contributions to one another so that they become separate from the rest of the group, forming a little subgroup. There will always be people in a group that we prefer but, as I said in Chapter 6, our role in any working group is not personal but professional. We are concerned only with the overall business objectives and therefore fulfilling the function of this particular group to the best of our ability. We must bring ourselves to the role to do this job effectively but not lose ourselves in petty preferences and defensive sociability, because this will cost the group.

Sabotage is where a member undermines the performance of the task by depreciating the contributions of others. The behaviour might look like sarcasm, repetitive negative criticism, political undermining behaviour both within and outside of the group or not sharing or contributing meaningfully to purpose and task.

Scapegoating is where the group gangs up against one member or someone outside of the group with strong hostility who then becomes the scapegoat. The person might then become the butt of the jokes, be mocked or derided, called names, put down or humiliated and get blamed for grievances or disappointments.

Step 3: Openness

Progress within the group can only be made as and when the members of the group open up and acknowledge these defensive mechanisms in operation; when they engage with the reality of what is actually happening between them and name the elephant in the room. De Board (1978) sums it up nicely:

> ... a group is able to function as a work group in which the members co-operate to achieve a common task and, because they are in touch with reality, develop and change as they succeed. Yet... the same group can [instead] behave as if the group had come together for pairing, for dependency or for flight or fight. In this mode, the group uses its energy to defend itself from its own internal fears and anxieties, and consequently neither develops nor achieves any effective output... [but] once the group faces reality, it realizes that it is facing itself and this causes its terrors and anxieties to flee, just as Oedipus by answering 'man' put the Sphinx to flight.

And so like Oedipus and the Sphinx the only way out of the pit is to face the beast and look him straight in the eye; by having the strength of character, each one of us, to face reality as it actually is, to face up to what is actually occurring within the group and to be willing to take back one's projections, shed light on the denials, heal the splits, refuse the introjections, stop the pairing and the scapegoating, let go of the narcissist and cease in the endless and repetitive need to please, collude or compete. Then real interconnectedness can arise and a tremendous amount of energy and creativity be made available as a resource for working to purpose and task.

The unconscious of the group carries its untapped creativity as well as the roots of its collective pain and if members can each have the strength of character to be with some of that pain, then that is when they will begin to really be able to collaborate with one another and to realize the combined potential of the group.

New skills and competencies required

In Chapter 3, I made the point that in corporate life our leaders and managers have not traditionally been developed, promoted or rewarded for this kind of competency and skill. Indeed, the Roads to Ruin research went on to recommend that further investigation be done on the relationship between this skill deficit at board level and 'the propensity to suffer major reputational crises'. People do so often want to do the right thing and speak up but the cultural constraints within an organization and the strength of collusion can be a powerful force stopping them from doing so. This is a point that organizations need to keep seriously in mind and one that I will come back to later in Part 3. For the moment, however, it is important to bear in mind that it can be very difficult to speak up in the face of strong interpersonal dynamics and that it is especially important, therefore, when addressing unconscious group processes that you have some robust and agreed frameworks in place.

The four that I recommend, in practice, are 'My Now', a variation of Exercise 3.1, which will help you to develop your emotional antenna before naming what it is that you might be sensing within the group. The second, 'Double Task', is for naming the elephant in the room. The third and fourth, 'Group Picture' and 'Sensing Matrix', use images and interconnectedness, as practical resources within the group, and are for the keener group practitioners.

EXERCISE 7.3 My now

When working within a group, begin consciously to practice the following three steps:

1 **Notice:** The first step is to notice and really feel your own reactions and allow them to be there. Accept them. Trust them. Breathe and do not push them away. To do so would create even more repression and denial.

2 **Inquire:** The second step is to put a little bit of distance between you and your experience in the group. Observe your experience with curiosity and a spirit of inquiry, not judgement. Oh that is what I am feeling; I wonder where that comes from and why? What triggered this response? Is it mine or does it belong to the group? Or is it telling me something about the group? Am I or others carrying projections or split off parts on behalf of the group as a whole? This will allow your default reactivity to loosen its tight grip on the situation.

3 **Choose:** The third step is to allow for some spaciousness in which to consider alternative ways of understanding and seeing the situation and perhaps alternative and more appropriate responses.

The more that you can practise these three steps, in all areas of your daily life, the more accessible they will become for you as tools when the heat is really on. Practise them, for example, in the privacy of your own home with your teenage children, or in the pub or restaurant when you cannot get served or indeed any group situation that provokes reactive patterns of response within you. This will help you to see your standard default position and, therefore, learn to separate what is real from what is unreal when trying to get the best out of any group.

EXERCISE 7.4 Double Task

Harold Bridger (1946) suggested that groups need to keep two differing tasks in focus. First, fulfilling the specific objectives and purpose assigned or agreed upon. Then, from time to time, suspending this first task, the business task and reviewing the dynamics within the group as they emerge. We call this the second task of reflection in action. I first came across this model when studying at the Institute of Group Analysis in London and later when working with the Grubb Institute (recently changed to the Guild 'in the business of now').

Take the following steps when working within a group:

Task 1: Identify the task that needs to be completed by the group and work towards completion of that task.

As well as:

Task 2: Periodically review the way in which the group is functioning and understand the processes operating within the group. Task 1 will be suspended from time to time in order to examine and review ways of working and managing interactions within the group.

Exercise 7.4 is not rocket science, but does it happen in practice within your working groups? I suspect not, if you are like most of the organizations that I come across. Any guesses as to why? The beauty of the model is that it allows for checks and balances. It requires group members to adjust and readjust where they are placing their focus and attention, from time to time, in order to consider how they could work more effectively within role and to purpose. Paradoxically, by speaking also to the group issues, as they are actually emerging, the model has the effect of helping to de-personalize the personal and the interpersonal elements. This is so important in terms of enabling an open level of curiosity and real inquiry as well as constructive dialogue. Bradford, Gibb and Benne (1964), in many ways the originators of this type of reflective approach, found in practice that:

> Group members, if they were confronted more or less objectively with data concerning their own behaviour and its effects, and if they came to participate non-defensively in thinking about these data, might achieve highly meaningful learning's about themselves, about the responses of others to them, and about group behaviour and group development in general.

The members of the group are then freed up to work in the here and now, with the reality of what is actually happening and as if the group itself were, as I said earlier in this chapter, some kind of separate additional iceberg, composed of an amalgam of the patterns of response and behaviours of all its members.

EXERCISE 7.5 Group picture

This exercise takes you out of your mind in order to see how you are picturing your working group or organization. It can be done alone or collectively, within a facilitated group. The use of an image and the arts enables a different kind of knowing to emerge, potentially leading to fresh insights and discoveries about the group and your place within it.

Take some art materials (the more the merrier) some paper, a working space and some time (maybe 30 minutes). Draw a picture of your group and place yourself within it. If possible, and without offering any explanation or interpretation yourself, try to get some feedback from trusted others/group members as to what they observe in your picture. Then consider the following questions:

- What insights (if any) did I gain from reflecting on the picture and other people's feedback about it?

- What was significant about how and where I appeared within it?

- Had anything important been omitted?

- What might the picture reveal about the group, the organization or the wider context?

EXERCISE 7.6 Sensing matrix

This exercise is primarily used for larger groups, of say 15 or more members. It invites the members to pay attention to dreams, overnight reflections and experiences and feelings in the body – this, as a way of exploring experiences of interconnectedness and the group unconscious.

The point of the exercise is to capture a deeper understanding of what might be emerging within the group and the wider context. As with brainstorming, all manner of new insights can reveal themselves and a remarkable amount of similarity between group members as to, heretofore unconscious, themes emerge.

Establish a start time when people need to be seated in silence on chairs, without desks, with a few chairs in the centre and the rest arranged as a series of outer concentric circles. Ensure that there is no talking or discussion. Just silence. Invite people to contribute, in a random fashion, by offering up their dreams, reflections, feelings or physical sensations, without any discussion or interpretation. They are to be offered as facts. Others do not respond, but instead contribute their own dreams, reflections, feelings or bodily sensation, as and when they choose.

After a previously agreed period of time has elapsed, perhaps 30–45 minutes, core themes and connections are discussed (for 15 minutes) in light of the purpose of the group overall. It is helpful if someone can have been previously appointed to facilitate that discussion, in which case it is best for them not to contribute during the first part of the session but instead to listen for themes and understandings as they emerge within the group.

Step 4: Wisdom

It will be essential for people working within and across groups within the new organizational paradigm to be able to stay in touch with the reality of their own performance. There are less and less specific job descriptions and guidelines available informing them how to do the job. And more and more, they, like the individuals that comprise them, must 'make the path by walking it'. The Grounding Steps framework will help any group to better connect with purpose, to develop insight and courage, to cultivate openness and curiosity and then, with this reflective awareness and wisdom, to exercise discernment in the face of the opportunities and challenges that present. It is clear that many of the cases described in the Roads to Ruin research would have benefited greatly from such a reflective approach or practice. It would have enabled the boards of companies such as Northern Rock and AIG to see more clearly the absolute fantasy of

FIGURE 7.3 The Grounding Steps framework – groups

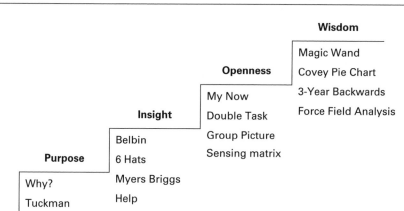

their seemingly relentless success in the market. That research concluded that:

> A number of the risk areas we identified predispose organizations to 'groupthink' or may be examples of its dangers where groupthink is defined as a psychological phenomenon that occurs within groups of people. Group members try to minimize conflict and reach a consensus decision without critical evaluation of alternative ideas or viewpoints.

The tools outlined in this chapter and summarized in Figure 7.3 are, in my view, the most effective way for any organization to monitor and manage that risk over time. They will enable any working group to stay present to what is actually occurring and to realize the depth of their almost unlimited, but heretofore untapped, creativity and resourcefulness. Never doubt that such a group could not change the world and certainly, in seeing more clearly, respond more successfully to what is being required of it and its members.

The power of the group

Organizational success is inherently built on the power and ability of the group to deliver to its highest level of performance. In earlier paradigms, we might have been operating within the context of a more fixed team with an appointed leader and clear guidelines in terms of purpose, task and role. Now, within the new organizational reality, we instead operate within and across a network of working groups. Cross-functional working groups are the new norm and their effectiveness largely dependent on the ability of the group to self-reflect in practice and for you, and each of its members, to take responsibility for their part in that process. In this changing context, to be effective means that you have to assume responsibility for developing the following competencies:

- EQ and a capacity for self-reflection;
- owning one's part in what is happening in any group;
- skill in facilitating free-flowing conversation;
- ability to articulate what is emerging in conversations; and
- sensitivity to group dynamics.

This concludes the first of my two-pronged framework, the personal and interpersonal as outlined in Chapters 4–7. In Parts 3 and 4 we will explore the second part of the framework, looking at the system and the wider context.

KEY POINTS

1 Groups have a life force of their own and the more that we can understand and engage with that, the more successful we, the group and the organization, will be in realizing its objectives.

2 Loose networks and cross-functional working groups are becoming the new norm and ensuring that there is sufficient clarity about purpose, intention and motivation will be critical to the performance of all group members.

3 Attending to the process of the group and, in particular, its defences against anxiety, requires courage and a new set of skills and competency on the part of group members.

4 Naming the elephant in the room will guard against the risks of groupthink and being out of touch with context and reality while at the same time freeing up a tremendous amount of energy that

can then instead be applied as a rich resource in terms of the completion of the task.

5 Organizational success is inherently built on the power of the group to deliver and possibly transform. As group members, we each need to be accountable for the part that we play in that.

PART THREE
System and context

The system
Working from the inside out

> *Masons, when they start upon a building,*
> *Are careful to test out the scaffolding;*
> *Make sure that planks won't slip at busy points,*
> *Secure all ladders, tighten bolted joints.*
> *And yet all this comes down when the job's done*
> *Showing off walls of sure and solid stone.*
> *So if, my dear, there sometimes seems to be*
> *Old bridges breaking between you and me*
> *Never fear. We may let the scaffolds fall*
> *Confident that we have built our wall.*
>
> **SEAMUS HEANEY**

Working from the inside out

In Part 1 we looked at the challenges that organizations are currently facing. We then went on to look, in Part 2, at the first part of the two-pronged approach, namely the personal and the interpersonal aspects of the workplace. This included specific tools and techniques that can help you to be more successful, as a person, within your role. The focus now, in Part 3, is on the second part of the two-pronged approach, namely system and context. This focus is critical because, as we have seen from some of the case studies outlined earlier, if purpose is unclear or communication poor, incentives mismatched to purpose or leadership unskilled, then no amount of self-actualization on the part of some key individuals, be they leaders or managers, will be sufficient to prevent a possible demise of the company. Attention is always needed to both sides of the model: the individual in terms of the personal and the interpersonal and the organization in terms of the system and the context.

In Part 4, we will look at governance and the responsibility that those who choose to lead organizations at the top have for addressing the issues outlined within this book and for adopting the two-pronged approach. We will look at the steps required to ensure that the business in question will continue to be that much more equipped for commercial success in a changing business landscape; that much more entitled to retain its licence to operate in the future and that much more likely to realize its fullest possible potential within society and the world. That being, in essence, the path to the enlightened organization.

Systemic thinking

It can be useful to think of an organization in terms of a system, with people and their activities being contained within a boundary that differentiates it from its environment and other systems. The boundary is the area where transactions take place within and between systems and between the organization and its surrounding environment. This brings into focus the significance of the managed interactions across those boundaries in terms of inputs and outputs, including the feelings and expectations of the people who work in, or receive services or products from, the organization.

It also draws attention to the nature of the boundary itself and whether it is open or closed and fixed or malleable. Just as a person can become cut off from others and from mobilizing their fullest potential, so too a system whose boundaries serve only to protect and differentiate it from other systems and context, rather than enable it to relate through these managed exchanges, will become a closed system cut off from reality and from meaning. The enlightened organization realizes that within the new reality, outlined in Figure 2.1, an increasingly sophisticated level of exchange is required across multiple stakeholder boundaries that are both malleable and semi-permeable. This will be vital if the organization is to network and interact successfully, learning from its context, from its interconnectedness and from what is emerging as its future.

The questions that need then to be asked of any organizational system are: 'What holds these people, resources and activities together?' 'What difference does it make?' and 'How does it continue to exist and prosper?' That will give you the purpose of the organization. Its purpose will ultimately define the boundaries while also providing the centripetal force around which its people and activities will coalesce. I referred to this earlier, in Chapter 2, in relation to the changing psychological contract at work and how, like atomic particles, the diverse elements of this new organic networked system will have a magnetic form of cohesion similar to the laws of attraction in science. As Jacques and Clement say: 'It is our values that make us, bind us together, push us apart and generally make the world go around'. (*Executive Leadership*, 1999)

The Grounding Steps framework

If, as suggested in Chapter 2, purpose, value and meaning are no less relevant for a whole organization than they are for its people, then the Grounding Steps framework might also be applied by it, as a tool to help navigate its way through this changing and at times turbulent environment. The framework will root the organization within its purpose and core strengths while also enabling it to remain open, flexible and responsive. It will enable it to then act wisely and with discernment within the context that it operates.

The first step of the Grounding Steps framework is concerned with purpose and why the organization exists in its current form; the second, with insight into its skills and the offerings that it provides; the third, with openness and the development of a spirit of inquiry; and the fourth and final step, with the resulting wisdom and discernment (see Figure 8.1).

We will look at each of the steps in turn, before examining in more detail the nature of your relationship as a person to the system as a whole. First, however, let me explain that we are focusing attention on the personal alongside the system, so that you can begin to see how aligned or misaligned they are (see Figure 8.2). The more alignment that there is, then the easier it will be for you to take up your role, as a leader or manager, and make a difference. And the more the system will be able to benefit and learn from its interactions with you. By contrast,

FIGURE 8.1 The Grounding Steps framework – system

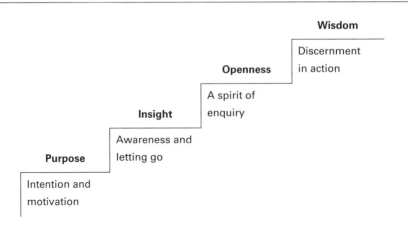

FIGURE 8.2 Person and system

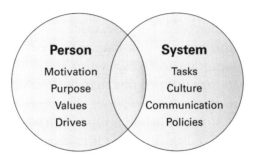

if instead, your purpose and values are opposed to that of the organization, or your mutual strengths out of sync or one or other of you is unable to remain open and curious about itself and the part that it plays
in the mutual co-creation, then the more difficult it will be for either
of you to perform at your best. You, for example, might have done all
the work in Part 2 of this book to help enlighten yourself about the
personal and the interpersonal aspects of your work but if the system
runs counter to your why, what and who it will remain a very difficult
challenge for you to take up a meaningful and effective role.

Step 1: Purpose

Organizational purpose and meaning provides the centripetal force
around which the systems, people, resources and activities coalesce.

It gives form and shape to the boundary of the system. Organizational purpose can be discovered, in part, by answering some of the questions outlined in Exercise 8.1.

EXERCISE 8.1 Why?

- What does the world need from us right now and in the future?
- Why do we exist?
- In what ways might we choose to meet this challenge and add value in the world?
- What values, if any, do we hold dear?
- What is our hearts' longing?
- What is the overall purpose of this organization?
- What activities are we engaged in right now?
- How are these related to our overall purpose?
- What will we receive as an organization if they are fulfilled?

Step 2: Insight

There are two elements to Step 2 and to developing organizational insight. First, appreciating what strengths the system has and what offerings it can provide. What is its core offering or USP (unique selling point)? Many of the tools and techniques outlined in Part 2 will be helpful in answering these questions. However, I have also added some additional questions below in Exercise 8.2.

EXERCISE 8.2 Our USP

- What core skills and talents do we possess?
- What gifts and offerings can we provide?

- What is our Unique Selling Point?
- What do we choose not to provide?
- Is there anything missing in terms of us fulfilling our overall and essential purpose?
- What known patterns of behaviour might stand in the way of our success?

Actual data about the organization's strengths and talents can be collected in many ways: by observation, for example, watching what people actually do in meetings and on the job; by reading written records, reports, speeches, charts or graphs; by interviewing people; and finally, by surveys, say a cultural audit or maybe structured questions that invite feedback from people in different parts of the system. Once key skills and talents have been identified, they should then be included as a systematic and integral part of all of the organizational policies so that they are reflected in everything from recruitment to recognition and reward.

The second aspect to developing organizational insight, as we saw with working groups in Chapter 7, is to be able to understand and work with potential blocks to performance and success. A system, just like a person, can develop strong templates and reactive patterns of behaviour. We saw this with some of the case studies outlined in earlier chapters. Take, for example, the financial crash where half of the major banks in the United Kingdom failed. These organizations failed by going against their customers' best interests and that of the public good. Yet they all blamed the interbank lending system. Some also blamed the rating agencies. Some, the regulators. In all cases, however, there was very little acceptance of the truth: namely that property prices go up and down and over the previous 60 years there had been three different sets of property failures. It was somehow easier for the banks to deny this and split off those parts of themselves that had performed badly than it was to accept the truth. Even since then, can we say that much has changed when we still have ongoing scandals? For example, in 2012 where some of the large banks were found to have been rigging Libor, the benchmark used by banks for borrowing in the London interbank market. Had they not got the message even by then or were their defensive patterns of unconscious behaviour just too deep?

An alternative example might be a recent client of mine. He was a paternalistic family owner/director who had big dreams for the company, wanting it to expand and grow in different markets. However, in working with him on why this change was not actually taking place, it became clear that he felt this need to overprotect his staff, as if they were members of his family, his children. Because of this he had been failing to make the tough decisions required and that would have enabled them to self-authorize and learn. His protective style of leadership was limiting the extent to which his 'children' could meaningfully contribute to co-creating the expanded business of his dreams. Only in seeing this pattern could he then let go, overcome the heretofore stagnant growth and enable the business to succeed.

Step 3: Openness

Here, at Step 3, we are seeking to develop a spirit of inquiry and curiosity about the organization as a system, including its subsystems, and the context within which it operates. What is it that the organization does not yet know or has not yet noticed about the emerging future that it is co-creating? Why does it need to find this out? Well, because the risk is potentially just too great if it doesn't. As Margaret Heffernan (2011) puts it:

> The sources of risk are interconnected, each amplifies the others. This means that organizations have to take a very concerted, coherent view of risk reduction and to consider social, intellectual, physiological, psychological and structural sources and remedies.

> We make ourselves powerless when we choose not to know. But we give ourselves hope when we insist on looking. As all wisdom does, seeing starts with simple questions: what could I know, should I know, that I don't know? Just what am I missing here?

Kodak and Sony are useful reminders of the need to stay current with the market and with what is going on. Kodak was a household name in the 1970s having sold its first consumer camera 100 years earlier. It was a pioneering electrical company that invented film and the first digital technology. Nevertheless, it failed to see how the market was moving increasingly towards the digital medium. Instead, it continued to focus on the older technologies that were being profitable for it at that time. The result was that others stepped in to capture the newly emerging market for digital technology and Kodak went into bankruptcy.

Sony engineers came up with the equivalent of the iPod before Apple but ran into obstacles within the company. This new technology was a threat to many of their existing product lines – including the big investment they had made in buying CBS Records. The engineering itself was not the challenge but reshaping the company strategy, organization and mindset was. Imagine a manager telling the people who had been working very, very hard on a portable CD player or integrating vertically with CBS Records that they were throwing significant parts of that away to try something new. That sort of conversation is difficult and painful. As in the case of Kodak, it was resisted and so Sony lost the huge opportunity that Apple seized. These are chastening stories, not of hubris but of the world changing around a stagnant brand. All the world's technology giants face the same risks, including – if not especially Apple – who, in launching a less than beautiful phone in 2013, instantly caused its share price to drop by 5 per cent. How do even Apple keep their almost reverent punters queuing at ungodly hours for yet another of their latest product updates, while whipping the media up into some kind of social frenzy?

If any organization is to flourish it needs to be paying keen attention to such matters and to what is actually going on both within the system and outside it. The exercises outlined under Openness in Chapter 7 will help it to do just this. These can be applied at the organizational level, although possibly within smaller subsystems who can then feedback their discoveries to the whole. These include Exercises 7.3–7.6 on pages 137–40.

Step 4: Wisdom

Organizations, as systems, need to develop increasingly sophisticated ways of transacting across semi-permeable boundaries with multiple stakeholders and within a turbulent changing environment. It takes courage and grace at times to determine which path to take. Should we go digital was the challenge presented to Kodak? Should we develop the iPod, the challenge for Sony? Should we launch a less than beautiful but cheaper phone in the recent case of Apple? These are tough decisions and the Grounding Steps framework can help organizations to work with the deep wisdom that arises from exploring the why, who and what questions first. It can help it to connect to its deeper purpose, intention and motivation. It can reveal its unique strengths and gifts as well as what patterns of behaviour might need to be let go of along the path. It can help it to cultivate a spirit of openness and inquiry about itself as a system, about its people and its subsystems and about the context within which it operates.

The enlightened organization, having worked with all three of those steps, finds itself then in a much better position to source wisdom and to exercise discernment; much more able to make explicit choices about the steps that it will now consciously take in order to embrace the challenges and opportunities that lie before it. To achieve this it uses the exercises outlined under Wisdom in earlier chapters, albeit applied at the organizational level and, where appropriate, through subsystems and then fed back to the whole.

The 'how' of this Step 4 does not just include actions to be taken in relation to the current organizational task; for example, whether to go digital or develop the iPod. It also refers to the multitude of things that need to be addressed internally, in terms of structures and supports, for any organization to flourish; for example, the communications policy or the incentive scheme. These are looked at more specifically below and in terms of the state of health of the system.

The health of the system and an Integral model

We have used the Grounding Steps framework to explore the why, who, what and how of the larger organizational system and to focus attention on the possible alignment or misalignment between person and system. We will come back to this question of alignment later in the chapter. First, however, I would like to present a balanced scorecard or methodology that can be used to drill further into the detail of the 'how' in Step 4 above, and help to create and maintain optimal health within the system. The reason for looking at this is two-fold. First, to see what kind of things need attending to in terms of leadership, culture and communication, for example if any organization is to flourish. The model provides a balanced scorecard of everything that needs to be addressed and, in that way, is a very helpful tool for ensuring balance and optimal health. Second, to make it quite clear that as and when these things are being dealt with effectively then you, as an individual, will be able to be much more effective in your role. However, to also point out that, if they are not being attended to appropriately then no amount of interpersonal effectiveness on your part will really help. In that sense the model highlights the supports that are required and necessary within the system itself in order for you to be able to take up your role effectively.

In systemic thinking, the organization as a whole is seen to reflect or mirror its parts, in terms of its people and subsystems. So that like holons, and some of the thinking around the new sciences that I outlined earlier in Chapter 4, one part of the organizational system will often demonstrate patterns of behaviour that replicate the whole, all the separate parts will be subtly influencing one another and paying attention to one part of the system will somehow invisibly impact and affect the whole. This is some of the thinking behind the Integral model developed by Ken Wilbur (the 'Integral' model'). The Integral model presents an overarching framework that combines several different approaches and theories about organizational consciousness and performance into one integrated way of viewing the whole. In

FIGURE 8.3 The Integral model

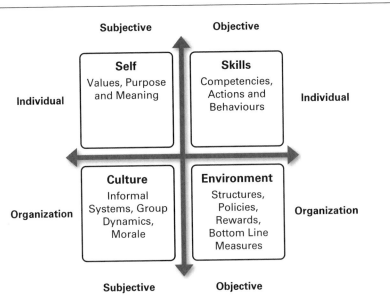

particular, it presents four different perspectives that one can have of any organizational system:

- The internal individual perspective – individual consciousness – personal values, identity, purpose and meaning.
- The external individual perspective – competencies, actions and behaviours.
- The internal group perspective – group consciousness – cultural values, relationships, group dynamics and trust and morale.
- The external group perspective – group social structures, systems, processes, policies and measures.

Preferences

The right sides of the quadrant are concerned with empirical observation. What does this organization do? The left side of the quadrants focus on interpretation. What does it mean? All four quadrants matter equally and influence one another. In practice, organizations, like you and I, are often skewed in favour of having a preference for one or other of the quadrants. Preference as a concept is described in Exercise 4.1 on page 54. In this context, it means that the organization has a habit of seeing itself primarily from the perspective of one of the quadrants. The consequences being, as Mark Twain pointed out, 'if the only tool that you have is a hammer, you will see everything as a nail'.

This might be demonstrated by the idealistic social service organization who has a preference for culture, the lower left quadrant. But, in paying more attention to the organization's cultural values, relationships and group dynamics, it ends up paying little or scant attention to the bottom right-hand quadrant, in terms of policies for payment, reward and measuring the bottom line. If this continues, the result will be that that the organization will possibly fail to bring in sufficient income for it to flourish and then not be able to develop and deliver the service that it could have otherwise meaningfully offered in the world. The Integral model instead helpfully forces it to redress this imbalanced preference by requiring that it pay equal attention to all four quadrants including its potential blind spot, the measurement of the bottom line.

It might be argued, in the case of the banks in the West, that the opposite was the case. That before the financial crash, significant amounts of attention were being paid to remuneration and reward while very little attention was being given to interpretation and the more subjective questions of what this and the figures really meant? So, less attention was being paid to the left hand side of the matrix. Then you could meaningfully ask how the directors of these large banks could possibly not have noticed what was happening within the culture of their organization? Well frankly, the answer might simply be that they were paying closer attention to something else – to the right-hand side of the model. Arguably they had become obsessed by their £50 and £60 million bonuses. Blinded by the figures, why would they seek to interpret? Would you have?

Part and whole

I will describe here some of the ways in which elements contained within the separate quadrants affect and impact the whole system and vice versa. In particular, I will look at culture (bottom left quadrant), change (top left), communication policies (bottom right), incentives and rewards (bottom right) and leadership skills (top right). I will also explain how the beauty of the Integral model, as a whole system approach, is that, notwithstanding that we might be focusing on one of the quadrants, the framework requires that we also engineer parallel shifts within the other three. It is for this reason that it can help you to keep your organization in a balanced and optimal state of health. For a more detailed examination of the quadrants, however, I would refer you to Ken Wilbur, *A Brief History of Everything* (1996).

Culture

Culture is at the bottom left quadrant. What does it mean in this context? The concept has been borrowed from anthropology and according to Edward Schein means the 'pattern of basic assumptions that a given group has invented, discovered or developed in learning to cope with its problems of external adaptation and internal integration. These have worked well enough to be considered valid and therefore, to be taught to new members as the correct way to perceive, think and feel in relation to those problems.'

This organizational ethnocentrism might be regarded as the organization's 'truth' or 'reality' or simply 'The ways things get done around here!' Paradoxically, at the moment within the City of London and many financial circles the panacea for all ills (meaning risk and damage to bottom line and reputation) that is being presented is culture. Just get the organizational culture right we are told and all will be well. A strong culture, it is said, will safeguard against behavioural risk. Again what does this – a strong culture – mean and how do you get one?

A strong culture is one that represents the values and dynamics that you could expect to see in an organization delivering the product or services that you supply; one that is congruent with that type of business and which would, therefore, promote its success. There is great value in analysing the current culture of your organization, contemplating one that is preferable, seeing where there are mismatches and then working to shape or mould the one that is preferred. This will necessarily also involve working systemically with all of the other three quadrants. First, for example, the top left quadrant in terms of attracting people to the organization whose values fit the 'new' culture. Second, the bottom right quadrant, in terms of rewarding behaviours in people that reflect the desired 'new' culture. Third, in terms of the top right quadrant, developing the skills and insight to be able to read and interpret the existing culture, identify more appropriate ones, assess the gaps between the two and ultimately intervene in ways that can best move and shape the organization accordingly.

The latter, leaders can do by being aware of the symbolic consequences of their actions and by attempting to foster the desired values but they can never control culture in the way that some banks and financial service organizations might be hoping. The holographic diffusion of culture means that it pervades activity in a way that is not amenable to direct control by any single group of individuals. Perhaps the banks are reacting to having been overly focused on the right hand side of the Integral model, thinking that now if somehow they could just get the culture right everything else in terms of personal values, leadership skills and incentives, for example, would be resolved. However, such a simplistic abdication to one quadrant alone is just another form of splitting and fails to appreciate the interconnectedness of the whole. As a policy it is likely to be as weak as the previous overreliance on the right-hand side.

The companies studied within the Roads to Resilience research (AIG, Drax Power, InterContinental Hotels Group, Jaguar, Land Rover, Olympic Delivery Authority, The Technology Partnership, Virgin Atlantic and Zurich Insurance) were all found to have worked hard on building and maintaining a strong culture, one that could adapt quickly. They did not just focus on building stronger and heavier defence mechanisms. The executive summary reports that these organizations built:

> The capability to deal with both expected and unexpected crises, while remaining focused on fulfilling the organization's purpose and protecting its integrity and reputation... risk exists at every level of the organization and lies within every decision made.

Change

The Integral model also provides a useful overview of how change can be effected through engineering parallel shifts in the four quadrants of the system (see Figure 8.4). Every organizational system will be unique in how it goes about this because there is no one-size-fits-all model available, more a framework to focus attention and understanding. The enlightened organization uses the Integral model to explore and find out what work needs to be done, knowing that change can only succeed if it is part of a whole system process. People change, not organizations, and people will not change how they operate if the underlying structures, processes and reward systems do not also change. Finally, the enlightened organization also recognizes that change will only succeed if the leadership team is committed to the work that will be required and to having the difficult conversations that Sony and Kodak, for example, failed to have. That means leaders and managers doing their work in terms of the system but also in terms of Part 2 of this book and their own personal and interpersonal effectiveness.

Communication

In a networked relational paradigm where people are potentially anxious and the operating environment is complex and changing, then communication becomes ever more critical as a tool for helping performance. News, as we saw in earlier chapters, can travel at the speed of light now. Good news, as well as bad, and it is beholden

FIGURE 8.4 The Integral model – change

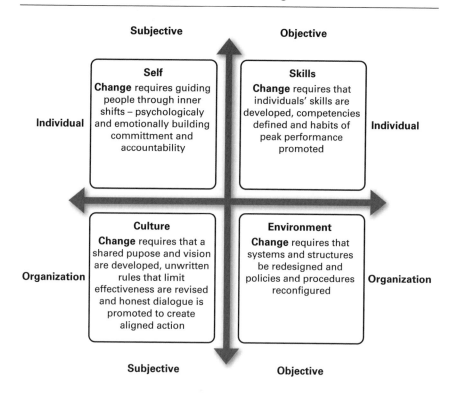

on any organization to safeguard itself against the wrong things being communicated either internally or externally. Perception being the new reality means that organizations can't be seen to be going off track even if in fact they are behaving perfectly. Furthermore, apart from any magnanimous gesture on the part of senior management, not involving key stakeholders in continuous communication excludes the possibility of tapping into the tremendous resource that they provide in terms of revealing new opportunities in the market place as well as determining improvements to practices and procedures. In fact, my desert island tool or resource for the enlightened organization, to replace Mark Twain's hammer, would be communication skills.

In terms of implementing the 'how' of Step 4 of the Grounding Steps framework and adhering to the systemic approach provided by the Integral model, a communication policy would be implemented and rigidly adhered to in terms of reward and recognition (bottom right quadrant). People in the organization, particularly leaders and managers, would be given the skills in how to communicate effectively about the organization and in a way that really represents its deep philosophy, purpose and meaning in the world (top right). The culture would be such that it truly supported those behaviours. It would invite diversity and practice inclusion, embracing dialogue, challenge and debate as rich resources within the system (bottom left). Finally at the level of the individual, values, purpose and meaning would be seen as critical in enabling people to become more accountable and thereby help to co-create the organization's future (top left).

This all sounds easy but it is not. An integrated communications policy takes time and a lot of effort. But it is critical to survival now. As David Whyte says: 'Conversation is not about the work; it is the work.' Too often the tendency can be for an organization to pick off some aspects of the policy leaving others behind. For example, I ran a programme for a large bank for over three years titled 'Courageous Conversations'. The aim was to teach leaders and managers within the organization to speak courageously about issues within the business. In theory, a great idea and it was a very successful programme for those hundreds of managers that attended over the three-year period. The problem was that the system could not fully support the value of the work by integrating it fully into the culture. This was because, at that time, the board and the top levels of management did not attend, as is so often the case with more senior levels of management. The problem then was that they were not themselves having meaningful dialogue and debate with one another. Nor were they providing an example of best practice and setting the tone from the top. So some very good work was done with those who attended the programme but the glass ceiling remained. Had the dots been joined by taking a whole system approach, the bank might potentially have been saved from a serious subsequent decline.

Earlier, in Chapter 2, we looked at some similar examples from the Roads to Ruin research. For example, the EADS Airbus A380 case where the difficult internal conversations were avoided by middle managers for six months which was when senior management found out about the then very costly problem of non-matching aircraft.

Perhaps today, such collusion would no longer occur. Perhaps people would be more willing to explicitly state what was already known at the time about the inability of the more senior levels of the organization to 'walk the talk' in the case of the bank and that the politically sensitive nature of the project was silencing middle management in the case of Airbus. But the tendency to split off like this and in a way abdicate the painful 'work' to another part of the system is something we saw in earlier chapters that runs deep as part of our very human defence mechanism. The bank's more senior managers were not bad or wrong and it was not a waste of time to do the work with those below. However, the benefit of an overarching framework is that it allows us to explore missing elements without laying blame and in so doing helps us to see the enormous additional value that could be realized if we were all to do the work on behalf of the whole system.

Incentives and rewards

Imagine the football player who is rumoured to be on a bonus, as part of his already enormous salary, for goals scored. How will that affect his game in terms of passing to other potential scorers? These are the type of concerns that preoccupy my nine-year-old son. As does whether cricketers should be allowed to wait for the umpire's call or walk. It is not that my son takes the moral high ground but more that I can see clearly how he is, as we all are, influenced by our very Pavlovian responses to what any particular system that we operate in provides us with in terms of recognition and reward.

It follows that if you really want to influence the behaviours, values and culture within any organization, you really do have to follow the money. That can involve some very tough decisions at times. Perhaps, as we saw with the BP incentives in Chapter 3, changing the bonus ratio from 70:30 for performance: safety to 70:30 for safety: performance. Perhaps, letting go of the solo performer senior lawyer who just will not collaborate with others, even if he or she is an excellent performer and rainmaker for the firm. Or perhaps letting the racist or biting footballer go if their behaviour is doing damage to the club's brand and reputation or is affecting the behaviour of others within the team. People can tolerate a lot if resources are low but unfairness in terms of policies about reward and recognition is felt and held deeply and does considerable damage to people's feelings of accountability and commitment.

The enlightened organization uses the Integral model to see where, at stage 4 of the Grounded Steps framework, it needs to have consistency and to demonstrate that visibly in order to support performance and again, without blame or the moral high ground, takes the tough decisions that are required in order to support the whole.

Leadership skills

Problems arise within systems often because of a failure of leadership to define, embody and defend organizational purpose and then to manage internal conflict. The unique task of leadership, therefore, independent of task and relationship skills, is the responsibility for scanning the Grounding Steps framework and the Integral model for gaps both formal and informal and then doing something about them. The task can be shared but it cannot be delegated. It is not the leader's role to know everything and fix everything but they should know where the trouble spots are and how these affect the whole. This requires systematic monitoring and the initiation of corrective action whenever the radar reveals a gap that threatens performance.

Person in system and role

It follows that you do not have responsibility for fixing the whole organization. However, it is important that you use these frameworks to help you to see more clearly the organization and its subsystems and where you sit within that. Decreasingly will you find your job description prescribed in advance as it might have been in the old hierarchical model. Instead now, within the newer organizational reality, the work to be done will reveal itself in an organic, emerging fashion and through the interconnecting patterns of the parts as well as the whole. In that sense, both of these models can help you to consider how, knowing what you now know about the organization, you could more meaningfully take up your role, working to purpose on behalf of the whole. How could you, in the words of John Bazalgette from the Grubb Institute, 'find, make and take up your role in the here-and-now'?

John Bazalgette and his colleagues Vega Zagier Roberts, Bruce Irvine and Colin Quine (2006) also helpfully point out that anyone who is willing to take up their role on the basis of their perception of contributing to the purpose of the system and who is willing to be held accountable for what they do is offering true leadership, notwithstanding where they sit within the organizational chart and Exercises 8.3 and 8.4 below are designed to help you to do just that. Leadership is no longer the preserve of those at the top.

EXERCISE 8.3 The Grounding Steps framework – person and system

See Figure 8.5 below and then answer the following questions.

- Using the Grounded Steps framework consider the answers to the questions why, who, what and how in respect of both yourself as a person and the system overall.

- What does this tell you about how the system is operating as a whole?

- Consider the possible alignments and misalignments between person and system.

- What have you learnt?

- What can you enquire about further?

- How can you now find, make and take up your role?

FIGURE 8.5 Person in system and role

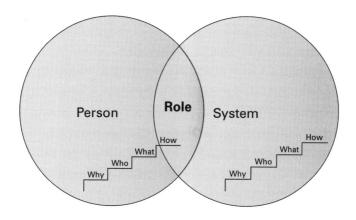

EXERCISE 8.4   The Integral model – person and system

- Taking your current operating system, write down what you notice and observe within all four quadrants of the Integral model.

- What does this tell you about what is or might be going on within each of the four quadrants?

- What does it tell you about how the system is operating as a whole?

- What have you learnt?

- What can you enquire about further?

- How can you now find, make and take up your role?

KEY POINTS

1   It is useful to think of an organization in terms of a system, with purpose defining the boundary which differentiates it from its environment and other systems.

2   Maintaining an effective system is the focus of the second prong of the two-pronged approach.

3   The Grounding Steps framework can root the system within its purpose and core strengths while also enabling it to remain open, flexible and responsive.

4   The Integral model provides an overarching framework that can help to keep the system in a balanced and optimal state of health. It highlights the internal supports that are required in order for you to be effective in role and that progress can be made by engineering parallel shifts in all of the four quadrants.

5   Both models can help you to see more clearly the organization as a system, as well as its subsystems, and then to consider how you might more meaningfully take up your role within that.

The context
Working from the outside in

09

We don't see things as they are, we see them as we are.
ANAIS NIN

I n the last chapter we looked at the nature of the organization from within and how it could be useful to view an organization in terms of a system with subsystems and a boundary differentiating it from its environment and other systems – the boundary being the point where transactions take place within and between subsystems and between the organization and its surrounding environment.

This led to thinking about the organization in terms of its whole and its parts, how each can mirror and reflect the other and how this distinction can help us, in a practical way, with frameworks that are designed to handle questions of meaning and taking action more discreetly. We also looked at the nature of the boundary itself. In reality, a system is only a mental construct. It does not actually exist in any tangible form and, while helpful as a concept, it can be unhelpful if we then make false assumptions about the boundaries being real and somehow fixed. As if they do, in fact, make us separate from the 'other' and our environment or as if they are actually set at a point in time in the relationship and forever thereafter immovable or unchangeable.

A system whose boundaries serve only to protect and differentiate it from other systems and context, rather than enable it to relate through these managed exchanges, will become a closed system, cut off from reality and from meaning. As I said in Chapter 8, the enlightened organization realizes that within the new reality, outlined in Figure 2.1, an increasingly sophisticated level of exchange is required across multiple stakeholder boundaries that are both malleable and semi-permeable. This will be vital if the organization is to network and interact successfully, learning from its context, from its interconnectedness and from what is emerging as its future. It is this larger context that is the focus of this chapter and the final part of the two-pronged approach.

The Context model

Context is an enormous idea. It encompasses just about everything and links closely to the theories about connectedness and wholeness that we looked at in Chapter 4. In part, it can be understood in terms of an adaptation of the work of Nadler and Tushman (1997) (The 'Context' model) in Figure 9.1.

Nadler and Tushman use a four-quadrant matrix, like Wilbur's Integral model which we discussed in Chapter 8, to describe the inner workings of any organizational system (see Figure 9.1). In that sense, their ideas mirror the distinctions already presented by Wilbur, of people, culture, tasks and formal systems. However, they then go further to outline issues relating to the context in which the organization

FIGURE 9.1 The Context model

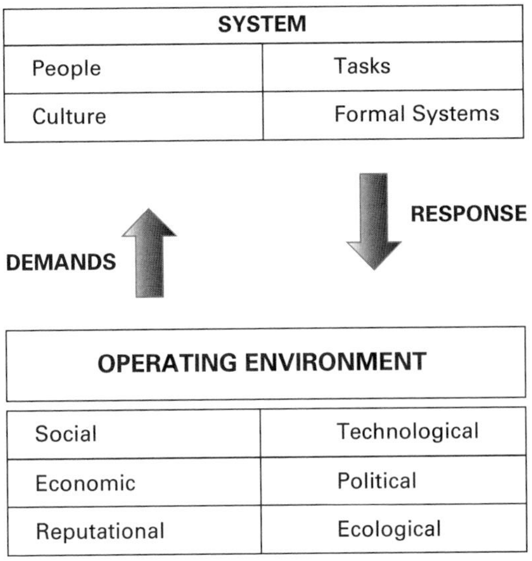

is operating and which are or might be relevant to its performance. These are presented by way of demands from the environment and then responses from the organizational system to those demands. The environmental demands might be social, technological, economic, political, ecological or reputational. As with the Integral model, we will all have our own unique preferences for what we choose to pay attention to in terms of the four quadrants within the systems boundary and in terms of the six outside, within the operating environment.

Looking first at the distinctions within the system, tasks includes the jobs to be done, the characteristics of the work itself, and the quantity and quality of the service provided. The formal system includes lines of accountability, the financial system, information services, monitoring and control mechanisms and job definitions. Culture drives the organization and relates to the people, the distribution of voice and power and can, as we saw in the last chapter, be characterized by 'the way we do things here'. Finally, people brings everyone's different skills, values, knowledge and experience, attitudes and behaviours into the equation to be matched with the formal and informal structures. These elements, bounded by the four boxes, represent the organizational system.

The world outside comprises social (expectations, attitudes, beliefs), technology (standards, support, developing technologies), economic (financial climate, competition for resources, budgets and cost control) political (policy, legislation, regulation), reputational (risks known and unknown that might affect brand value) and ecological (green issues). These represent the operating environment within which the organization has to operate.

The world outside is completely indifferent to what happens inside our four organizational boxes. We use these ourselves to concentrate our efforts on what it is that we can do as a system. However, exactly what we do with these resources is governed entirely by the demands and responses determined by the world outside. This is the only legitimacy for the existence of the organization. So our survival is not certain. What we need to make sure of is that we have the resources, skills and attitudes available to us so that we can increase the probability that we will experience a particular outcome, depending on the investment we make through our effort (salient to us) and performance (salient to our customer or client). The environment will make a judgement of the response comparing this with demands.

In short, the context is completely indifferent to what happens inside the organization unless it influences the responses to demands.

It is useful to remember this in business. There is no entitlement to success. The alchemy of success comes from engaging meaningfully with your context and trying your very best with the resources that you have internally. Certainly, the enlightened organization is both vigilant and respectful of the power of its context to enable it to either flourish or die and does its utmost to reconfigure its organizational boxes in a way that meets the real demands of the context.

I think that one of the reasons that the general public became so angry in Europe after the banks crashed was that they felt that some of the banks should have been left to die. Instead, they were allowed to be rescued, with taxpayers' money, in breach of one of the basic tenets of the capitalist market and one that the banks themselves were fully cognizant and a willing part of: namely that you take risks in business and finance and suffer the consequences. Otherwise, how do you remain respectful, vigilant and discerning? It can be seen as all very complicated but you know it can also be altogether simple. In a pure Context model, senior bondholders in organizations like Anglo Irish Bank would have simply lost their money. The wider European context was fearful, however, that this would lead to a sovereign default. And so the wider context became relevant. Should it have? Where in this global interconnected age can we draw the line? These are some of the challenges that we now face in a world where organizational impact crosses boundaries in every sense of the word.

Interconnectedness

It might be tempting, as we saw in Chapter 4, to seek some kind of closure, some smaller place that we can inhabit, imagining ourselves to be still somehow separate and distinct both as an individual and as an organization. However, that would be to ignore the systemic reality that we are all, in effect, deeply connected and interdependent. The skill is in being able to operate with a semi-permeable boundary that lets reliable information about what is happening in the world outside back into the system. Where you begin and end is also a question because connectedness is not a linear phenomenon.

Maybe, for example, the seeds of greed and entitlement were planted back in 1990 when in the United States the Glass-Steagall Act was, in part, repealed. This had regulated the mortgage market and was then considered to be making it more restrictive for poorer people to access housing. In an attempt to make it easier for them to buy homes parts of the act were repealed. Counterintuitive, I know, to say that that was the start of the problem, but that is the way that context can often work with time.

As Thich Nhat Hanh (1991) said, 'All things depend on all other things for their existence. Take, for example, this leaf... Earth, water, sea, tree, cloud, sun, time, space – all these elements have enabled this leaf to come into existence. If just one of these elements was missing, the leaf could not exist. All beings rely on the law of dependent co-arising. The source of one thing is all things.'

The leaf does not arrogantly think that it did it all by itself, unlike some rather defended organizational systems that I can think of. There is a dance required and organizations need to really stay in touch with the moves if they are to survive and flourish in the longer term. They need to keep up with their environment in all sorts of unusual ways. The Roads to Ruin research case studies, some of which are outlined in Chapter 2, tell stories of many businesses that became separate and defended and then lost touch with the complex context within which they were operating, misjudging the risks that were inherent in their business model. Remember also the examples of Kodak and Sony from the last chapter. Each of these companies missed the strong patterns that were emerging in their market place and instead focused intently on the relative safety of the technologies that they already knew. By contrast, I mentioned briefly in the introduction the companies Amazon and Starbucks, each of which recently voluntarily elected to pay additional tax in the United Kingdom, where they have one of their largest consumer markets. Why? Because there was an increasing demand from their public, albeit not a legal requirement, and they felt the need to respond.

The companies that were studied as part of the Roads to Resilience research were discovered to have developed exceptional radar, which enabled them to gather intelligence from multiple sources and across a myriad of boundaries, collating different types of information, both formal and informal, and then responding effectively in a controlled and considered manner.

Purpose

The Context model also calls into question the issue of how to agree and decide on the purpose of the organization. It raises the question as to whether we can do this from within the four boxes that define and differentiate it as a system. Or do we have to answer the question from without? Can purpose only be truly defined from the outside, from the context, because it is only in looking outside of ourselves, as a system, to the demands of the environment that we can really ever understand what will be required of us in response? This idea links back to notions of a calling or purpose that we looked at in Chapter 4 and gives a new way of looking at the why question from the Grounded Steps framework. It also resonates with the work of Peter Senge and Otto Scharmer on Theory U (2009). Theory U describes a journey of change much like the transition curve that we looked at in Chapter 1. The distinction being, however, that it makes more explicit in the second half of the journey the idea of sensing purpose from outside, allowing and letting purpose come to reveal itself to us.

Perhaps though, even the question of inside the system or outside the system is to force a dichotomy between either/or that does not in fact exist. System and context are themselves also so inextricably interconnected and interdependent that maybe we should not be thinking in terms of either/or but instead of both/and. Perhaps it is the synergistic alignment of the forces and energy of both that actually defines purpose. Purpose in that sense can never be static. Nor can it be articulated in advance. Instead it needs to be calibrated and recalibrated, as required, so that it can be discovered and rediscovered as the context changes and changes, again and again.

Ways of seeing

The problem is exacerbated by our inability to see things clearly and as they truly are. For example, do we view our context in terms of presenting opportunities or threats? Is our cup half full or half empty? Any answer to this will be largely given by the templates that we formed at an early age, and outlined in Chapter 4; and by whether we see the world as a benign, helpful loving place or one where resources are scarce and being in business necessarily means 'survival of the fittest'.

In reality both views can be true. Old resources diminish. New ones arise. Changes in context remove old sources of meaning and resources but also, even at the same time, open up new possibilities, new directions, and new meanings. It is one of the critical roles of leadership now to discover, reveal and embody those new meanings. What is the meaning of this work, this organization in the current context, and how can we best respond? This is because the organization has to be vigilant and awake to notice these subtle shifts in context and make adjustments accordingly. You can only do this if you are able to step out of your unconscious templates and view your organization from outside its frameworks and ideologies so that you can then observe its limitations and defects and re-author a more comprehensive view. Like Aikido and most martial arts, the skill starts with first knowing when you yourself have gone off balance and then being able to get back to centre before your opponent does. As with step two of the Grounding Steps framework, the critical work starts with self; knowing your strengths as well as your deeply held patterns of response that come along regularly and knock you off centre.

Learning to see the whole, system and context, is extraordinarily difficult and traditional analytical ways of measuring will not help. Analysis narrows our field of awareness and actually limits our ability to experience the whole symbiotic relationship. The openness practices described earlier, in Chapters 7 and 8, under step three of the Grounding Steps framework are designed to help here. They will take you to another deeper and more knowing place within you, where what is occurring in the relatedness between system and context can in many ways make itself known to you. All manner of insight and new information can reveal itself to you when you are able to simply let go and be present in this way – present to what is actually occurring. This relates to the work of Senge and Scharmer on Theory U, namely learning to sense more deeply and, in doing so, allow information that is relevant to come to you.

Like sex and falling in love this is not really something that can be told. It must be experienced first-hand to appreciate its power and, as I have explained in earlier chapters, any process can work for this that encourages non-linear thinking and intuition. For that, it helps greatly to use alternative forms of expression such as meditation, walking, dance, drama, art, stories, music, colour and images. The list is endless but the critical task is to evoke your senses not your mind. This will also help you to self sooth and operate from within the parasympathetic system, so that your familiar threats and drives do not then cloud your vision, driving you back to reactive patterns of anxiety that will endlessly blind you to the bigger picture and what it is that might actually be occurring.

Seeing the whole can be difficult within any context, not just business. For example, we ask ourselves now how so many people colluded with the abuse of children by the church and some well-known television personalities in the United Kingdom. What were we not seeing then that we can see now? What could people not say and had to repress back then? What are we ourselves not seeing now that to our children will be completely obvious in time? Perhaps that we are destroying our planet with our insatiable appetite for consumerism? Or, that anxiety disorders in young children are worryingly on the increase and will lead to a significant review of teenage education in time. Or that we can fly to the Moon! As Margaret Heffernan (2011) said: 'As all wisdom does, seeing starts with simple questions: what could I know, should I know, and that I don't know? Just what am I missing here?'

A biological perspective

If system and context are in many ways one then we can invite a biologist's perspective of the organization as an organism in search of sustenance co-existing in a symbiotic relationship with its environment. The ease with which sustenance can be won relates to how rich and abundant the resources are relative to the requirements or needs of the system. This relatedness, the one with the other, is then a living dynamic relatedness that is complex, changing and vital at all times.

A biological paradigm suggests that organizations, being shaped by their context, are an integral part of all of co-creation. In the enlightened organization, you might therefore come to see that:

- its purpose is unique and potentially limitless and often paradoxically more easily answered by listening to the context and what might be required of it in the world;

- it is not simply the sum of its outputs but perhaps has a broader purpose which is to enable its context and the people operating within it to fulfil their potential in the world;

- barriers between competing elements within the business can be destroyed and replaced with a sense of common work to be done;

- diversity and inclusion bring challenge, conflict and debate all of which are critical resources within the organization;

- being intricately connected to the world outside it would be best to follow a simple rule whereby you treat all stakeholders (including, for example, customers, suppliers, competitors, governments and distributors) that you interact with as part of yourselves, and seek the best for all involved parties, then your organization would benefit the most; and

- that the real purpose of the organization is only achieved over time and that a longer-term perspective will create success in both the longer as well as the shorter term.

Person in system and context and role

I mentioned in Chapter 7 that problems arise within systems often because of a failure of leadership to define, embody and defend organizational purpose and manage internal conflict. Problems also arise because leaders and managers cannot see clearly the forces and factors at play within their operating environment. Kegan and Lahey (2009) suggest that to be able to do this one needs leadership of a different sort: leadership that leads to learn, that can hold the and/ or contradictions of systemic living, that can problem-find and that can take a meta-position while operating interdependently. These are some of the skills that we looked at in Chapter 3 as being a requirement for the enlightened organization.

The unique task of the more senior levels of leadership therefore, independent of task and relationship skills, is the responsibility for scanning the Integral model and the Grounding Steps framework for problem areas and doing something about them. It is also to integrate the Context model so that questions about the environment become part of daily practice, as does trying to answer some of the more important questions from the outside in. Again, as I said in the last chapter, this task can be shared but it cannot be delegated. Nobody does this high-wire act exactly right, but to the extent that it is done at all, a formal organization may in practice be informally leaderless.

The focus of other types of leadership has, of course, moved down throughout the organization with people at all the varied levels interconnecting meaningfully and purposefully with the outside global context. Each of these ambassadors for the organizational system needs too to be fully engaged in the inquiry as to what the world requires from this organization at this point in time and for the future. In the enlightened organization, we will each of us move in and out of this leadership and followership role, as and when the context prescribes. This is because the product or service to be supplied will no longer always be known in advance but instead emerge through web-like networks of interconnected and interdependent relationships and possibly at any level and at any point of entry to the system.

So, as I said before in Chapter 8, anyone who is willing to take up their role on the basis of their perception of contributing to the purpose of the system in context and who is willing to be held accountable for what they do is offering true leadership, notwithstanding where they sit within the organizational chart, and Exercises 9.1 and 9.2 are designed to help you to do that.

EXERCISE 9.1 The context

- Taking your current operating system, write down what you notice and observe within all four quadrants (people, culture, task and formal systems) of the Context model.

- Write down or draw what you think is present, emerging and potentially relevant under the six environmental headings: social, technological, economic, political, reputational and ecological.

- What does this tell you about the demands from context on the system?

- How might these demands inform its core purpose?

- What does it tell you about how the system is operating in practice?

- What does it suggest in terms of alternative possible responses?

- What have you learnt?

- What can you inquire about further?

- How can you now find, make and take up your role within the system and the context?

FIGURE 9.2 The domains

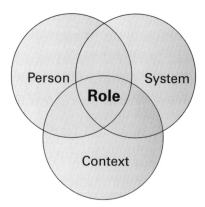

Vega Zagier Roberts, John Bazalgette (2006) and their colleagues at the Grubb Institute speak of the three domains in Figure 9.2 and how taking up one's role means to take action that furthers the purpose of the system in its context. Being effective in role requires one to integrate one's experience from each of the three domains of person, system and context, integrating motivation, purpose and resources to determine one's behaviour. They add:

Perhaps another way of understanding the... domains is about different levels of accountability: accountability to oneself (values, beliefs, needs, desires); to one's system (to contribute to purpose); to the wider context (community, society); and to something else – humankind, life, cosmos, God?

I will leave the *something else* for a later book but accountability is something that we will look at briefly and to close in Chapter 10: accountability in terms of governance and the responsibility of those in charge of any organizational system to nurture and take care of for the future.

Meanwhile, and as we come to the end of this part and my two-pronged approach, I want to finish by restating that attention must be paid to the personal and interpersonal as well as to the system and the context and that only parallel shifts in both (prongs) can enable progress. The enlightened organization is the one that commits to this approach and is willing to do the parallel work that is required on behalf of the system as a whole in the service of its context. But the enlightened organization cannot read this book. Only you can. It follows that knowing what you now know about:

- yourself as a *person*, about working with others and within groups from Part 2 of this book;
- the organization as the *system* from Chapter 8; and
- the operating environment as the *context* from this chapter.

How could you now find, make and take up your role working to purpose and on behalf of your organization?

EXERCISE 9.2 My role

See Figure 9.2 and knowing what you now know about:

- yourself as a *person*, about working with others and within groups from Part 2 of this book;
- the organization as the *system* from Chapter 8; and
- the operating environment as the *context* from this chapter.

How could you now as a person and in this current context find, make and take up your role working to purpose and on behalf of the system?

KEY POINTS

1 An organizational system whose boundaries serve only to protect and defend will become a closed system cut off from context, reality and meaning.

2 The Context model describes both system and context and shows how indifferent context is, in reality, to what happens within our organizational boundaries.

3 Context does not care for anything other than our response.

4 Organizational survival is not at all certain. However, it is much more assured if we can stay fully interconnected and respond appropriately as an organization to the demands of the operating environment.

5 Organizational purpose is defined from outside the organization as well as within and needs discovering and rediscovering as the context invariably changes.

6 Learning to see the whole, system as well as context, is extraordinarily difficult and the openness exercises contained within this book will help you to do that.

7 The two-pronged approach requires that attention be paid to the personal and interpersonal as well as to the system and the context and only parallel shifts in both (prongs) can enable progress.

8 We each need to think carefully about how best to take up our role in a way that enables us to be accountable for ourselves (in terms of values, beliefs, desires and needs), our system (in terms of contributing to purpose), and the wider context (in terms of our community and the wider society).

9 The enlightened organization is the one that commits to this approach and is willing to do the parallel work that is required on behalf of the system as a whole in the service of its context.

PART FOUR
Governance

Governance and the enlightened organization
Directing performance for the longer term

10

And a woman who held a babe against her bosom said, 'Speak to us of Children.' And he said:
Your children are not your children.
They are the sons and daughters of Life's longing for itself.
They come through you but not from you,
And though they are with you, yet they belong not to you.
You may give them your love but not your thoughts.
For they have their own thoughts.
You may house their bodies but not their souls,
For their souls dwell in the house of tomorrow, which you cannot visit, not even in your dreams.
You may strive to be like them, but seek not to make them like you.
For life goes not backward nor tarries with yesterday.
You are the bows from which your children as living arrows are sent forth.
The archer sees the mark upon the path of the infinite, and He bends you with His might that His arrows may go swift and far.
Let your bending in the archer's hand be for gladness;
For even as he loves the arrow that flies, so He loves also the bow that is stable. **KHALIL GIBRAN**

Corporate governance has come into the spotlight in recent years as we all learn lessons from the financial crisis. The UK Corporate Governance Code (2010) defines its purpose as 'to facilitate effective, entrepreneurial and prudent management that can deliver the long-term success of the company'. The Tomorrow's Company Good Governance Forum, which works to support large, mainly commercial organizations, defines it (2012) as: 'The procedures and practice associated with decision-making, performance and control, which provide structures and satisfy expectations of accountability...'

The concept of governance is not, however, confined to the financial sector or large commercial organizations. Every organization, no matter what its size or purpose, will have someone or some group of people that take active responsibility for its direction and future and for the effectiveness of its decision making and management processes. The difference is that an organization that is registered in law, as a limited company, will assume legal responsibilities towards its stakeholders. In the case of a large commercial company that is listed on a stock exchange, this primarily means the shareholders, who invest in the company by buying its shares. In so doing they help to fund its varied activities, enabling the organizations to do business and grow. In law, the shareholders are entitled then to rely on those that are appointed as directors of the company to fulfil that task to the best of their abilities.

Often a large amount of legislation can develop in an attempt to regulate this fiduciary duty of care. This is because many investors are people, like you and I, who are hoping to put some money away in a pension and have it 'work' for us until we retire. We are then completely reliant on those who take this money to safeguard it for us. Different countries will have different levels of restriction in place and a company when choosing to list in, say, New York, Hong Kong or London, for example, will be factoring that into its decision about location. The investor too, in that the more heavily regulated the location, then arguably the more protection afforded to it as a shareholder.

Like everything in commerce a balance needs to be struck between inviting investment into the country of location and protection from risk. Often legislation will develop in a piecemeal fashion, as new issues emerge and new forms of protection or relaxation are required.

In France, for example, much of the legislation is contained in the French Commercial Code and the Monetary and Financial Code. In the United Kingdom and Ireland, it is mainly within the Companies Act 2006 and in the United States, significant provisions are contained in the Securities Exchange Act 1934, the Sarbanes-Oxley Act 2002 and the Glass-Steagall Act that I referred to in Chapter 9. In nearly all countries, however, regardless of the specific location or legalization, protection is mostly afforded by holding directors personally liable where:

- the company has gone into insolvent liquidation; and
- prior to winding up the director knew, or ought to have concluded, that there was no reasonable prospect of the company avoiding insolvency; and
- the director fails to establish that he or she took every step to avoid loss to creditors.

One of the reasons that there is still so much anger directed towards the banks in Europe is that none of the directors went to jail, notwithstanding that many must have acted illegally. There has been no closure for the public who, by and large, ended up footing the bill. These directors breached the law by trading 'wrongfully' because they continued to do business and sign off their accounts as a 'going concern' when in fact their banks clearly weren't. None of these directors were held personally accountable for the devastation that subsequently ensued and the enormous cost that this brought to an ever-widening group of stakeholders. Unlike Ken Lay and Jeff Skilling in the United States, they were not jailed, even for wilful blindness, a charge that while they might not have known that their organization was insolvent, they should or could have done so. The actual cost of this catastrophic event is probably more or less impossible to say but some estimates are in the region of $25 trillion. Hopefully, the pain that it has created, within all parts of our society including the banks, will not be in vain and the lessons learnt from it such that this behaviour would neither occur nor be tolerated again in the future.

In the case of public sector organizations and charities, there are often, paradoxically, more stringent governance regulations. There the need is to protect taxpayers and those who fund the organization's activities as well as more vulnerable client stakeholders such as the patients, children and other users of the services. Ultimately, though, regardless of what type of organization you are considering, governance is always about directing the longer-term performance of that organization and thereby safeguarding the interests of all its stakeholders. It is increasingly about taking the steps required to ensure that the business in question is that much more equipped for success in a changing complex landscape; that much more entitled to retain its licence to operate and that much more likely to realize its fullest possible potential within society and the world. Those of us who take on the role must be responsible and accountable accordingly.

The theory applied and a recap on the two-pronged approach

Systems as usual

Any person or group of people with responsibility for directing the longer-term performance of an organization is holding a governance position. These people will typically be termed governors or directors and will work together on what is termed a board, as board members. The board, like any system, will have a boundary to differentiate it from other sub-systems within the organization and from its environment. That boundary will be given by the purpose of the board, which is itself given by answering the following questions: 'What holds us together?' 'What difference do we make?' and 'How and why do we continue to exist and prosper?'

In that sense, it is systems as usual and all of what I have said in Chapter 8 applies equally to a board. There we looked at how the Grounding Steps framework can help a system to navigate its way through changing and unknown waters. It can root a board in its purpose and core strengths while also enabling it to remain open, flexible and responsive. Ultimately, if applied, it can enable a board to discern the better path to follow and to make explicit and conscious choices about the steps that its organization needs to take in order to better embrace the challenges and opportunities that lie before it. In Chapter 8, we also explored Wilbur's Integral model as an overarching systemic framework. This too can help a board to keep its organization in a balanced and optimal state of health. Finally, in Chapter 9, we saw how any system has to be mindful of its context and this, of course, has to be especially true for any board where the role is, in part, being the strategic eyes and ears of the organization.

The two-pronged approach

In Part 1 of the book, we looked at how:

- complexity and change are affecting the way in which organizations are able to do business in the world;
- new organizational structures are emerging;
- brand and reputation have assumed a critical level of importance; and
- the role of leaders and managers in adapting to all of this is key.

I offered the two-pronged approach as a way of responding to these challenges and building the enlightened organization. The two-pronged approach requires that attention be paid to the personal and interpersonal as well as to the system and the context and suggests that only by creating parallel shifts in both can real progress occur (see Figure 10.1). The two prongs are:

- the personal and interpersonal, in order to see where, in the midst of the endless complexity and change, we might be blocked professionally and creatively and how, in working skilfully with this insight and awareness, we could reclaim and unleash our own purpose, passion and potency; and
- the organization, more broadly, in terms of systems and context so that we can, like the goldfish in the bowl, understand and see the nature of the water that we are actually swimming in, and therefore make more intelligent choices in stepping forth and shaping our collective business path.

FIGURE 10.1 The two-pronged approach

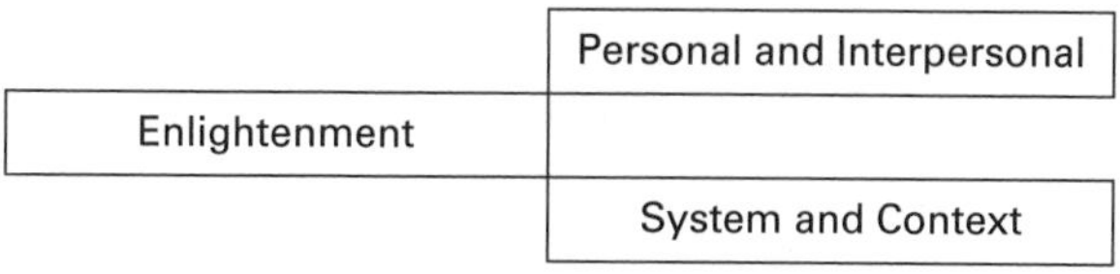

Board members need to attend to the work required within each of the two prongs. They need to investigate the personal and interpersonal as well as the system and context, without preference for one over the other and at all times balancing and fine-tuning elements within each. In short, this means their doing the work required within Parts 2 and 3 of this book.

Personal and interpersonal

In Part 2, we looked at the fact that humans are not, by their nature or design, rational beings. Often they are reactive, especially when working under pressure. They can respond defensively to people and the task, which leads to them underperforming. In addition, we saw how feelings of separation can also hinder personal performance. The increasing amount of pressure on board members is great, as unknown risks emerge, public awareness grows and brand and reputation are adversely and instantly affected. Furthermore, the very nature of their role is somewhat isolated and separate. It follows that, because of this increased anxiety and possible isolation, an understanding of the irrational nature of being human might be particularly relevant for them in terms of addressing their own underperformance.

In Chapters 5, 6 and 7, I introduced the Grounding Steps framework and provided a variety of exercises to enable personal and interpersonal effectiveness. These exercises are just as relevant for board members as they are for any other members of the organization, if not indeed more so. This is because they, of all sub-systems, need to be able to perform effectively as a group both in order to do the strategic work required of them at this level as well as to establish and maintain the right tone throughout the whole of the rest of the organization. Boards set the tone and it was a lack of competence in this area, at board level, that led to the following observation in the Roads to Ruin research:

> A valuable question for further investigation in this area is whether there is a causal link between weaknesses in leaders and board composition with respect to the so-called 'soft' [personal and interpersonal] skills and the propensity to suffer major reputational crises.

As outlined in Chapter 2, this research studied crises affecting 21 organizations with pre-crisis assets of over $6 trillion. One of the key findings was that the functioning of the board itself can pose a significant risk to governance. Most of the organizations had been well regarded and many had good reputations. Only a few emerged without obvious immediate damage. Six collapsed and, while three of these were revived, this was achieved through a state rescue and/or what amounted to a nationalization. Most suffered large, uninsurable losses and their reputations were severely damaged. Finally, the position of most chief executives, chairmen and many board members was put into question. Where were they, personally and interpersonally, that they could have allowed this to occur? Was it ignorance, wilful blindness or corruption?

System and context

In Part 3 we looked at system and context and how the unique task of the more senior levels of leadership, independent of task and relationship skills, is responsibility for scanning the Grounding Steps framework, the Integral model and the Context model for problem areas and doing something about them. The responsibility for this lies ultimately with the board, because board members are themselves accountable to stakeholders. The three models provide the checks and balances required by the second prong of my two-pronged approach and will enable any board to build a more enlightened organization. No board will do this high-wire act exactly right, but to the extent that it is done consistently, they will find themselves on the right path.

Grounding Steps framework

The Grounding Steps framework can be applied by the board to itself, as a system as well as to the whole organization. In that sense, the board wears two hats. The exercises set out in Chapter 7 can be used by it when looking at its own group functioning and the exercises in Chapter 8 when looking at the wider organizational system. This means that in terms of addressing purpose, the board's 'why' will be discovered in response to the questions outlined in Exercise 7.2 and the organization's 'why', in response to the questions outlined in Exercise 8.1.

Insight too can be looked at in terms of the board as a sub-system and in terms of the organization as a whole. The first, by looking at the skills and strengths that individual board members bring and completing the relevant exercises in Chapters 5, 6 and 7. The second, by answering the questions outlined in Exercise 8.2 on pages 151–52. However, the board will also need to attend to potential blocks to performance and success – its own and that of the organization. Systems, like people, as we saw in Chapter 8, have blind spots and defensive, reactive patterns of response and these need attending to just as much as the strengths. This is covered, more specifically, under 'Blindness, wilful or otherwise, on the board' below.

Openness is critical at this level of thinking, where the task is primarily about creating strategies that will enable the longer-term performance of the organization. Arguably, it is therefore one of the key functions of board members to remain curious and enquiring about existing practices within the organization as well as keenly attentive to what is potentially going to be required of it in the future from without. This so that adjustments can be recommended and made. The exercises outlined in Chapter 7 will help board members to flex that muscle. These include Exercises 7.3 and 7.6 on pages 137 and 139–40.

Finally, wisdom comes from applying the previous three steps and then enabling parallel shifts to occur within the two-pronged model.

Integral model

The Integral model, described in Chapter 8, provides a board with a four-quadrant balanced scorecard with which to measure and improve organizational performance. The right sides of the model, skills and environment, are concerned with formal and empiric observation. The left, self and culture, with more informal subjective interpretation. The model helpfully redresses any potential prefer-ence that a board or organization might have for one quadrant over another by requiring that it pay equal attention to all four.

Context model

The Context model, described in Chapter 9, requires board members to ask questions about the operating environment, ensuring that it becomes part of their regular practice to answer the important stra-tegic questions from the outside in.

Blindness, wilful or otherwise, on the board

In the Introduction, I spoke about wilful blindness, a legal term that means being accountable for something that you may not have known about but that you could or should have known. I also put forward the proposition that we must each make a conscious choice about whether we want to be able to see or not; to see what is really going on so that we can help our organizations respond appropriately.

Nowhere is this more acutely true than at board level. Yet one of the key findings of the Roads to Ruin research was that the functioning of the board itself can pose a significant risk to governance. Let me highlight some potential areas of board risk, before outlining what I mean by the enlightened organization and what a privileged role it is to be able to play a part in realizing that.

A closed system

We saw in Chapter 9 that if a system has too strong a boundary, one that seeks to protect and differentiate it from other systems and the context, rather than enable it to relate through these managed exchanges, it will become a closed system, cut off from reality, feedback and learning. The danger then being that it does not take in valuable information from its context and learn how to better organize itself in response. It operates, instead, from the fantasy of what might be required by its operating environment rather than what is actually required. Ultimately it runs the risk of failure if it remains so out of touch. This is what happened with many of the boards in the Roads to Ruin case studies. Their early warning systems, in terms of the people who could see what was actually going on, was in many cases silenced and in many others ignored. Airbus and Enron, described in Chapters 1 and 2, provide significant examples of where this occurred.

This will always remain a problem unless and until board members reach out and seek the information that they need and are visibly seen to do so. Otherwise, human nature is such that while people might want to speak up, the forces against and risks of fallout are so great that most of us will apparently choose not to do so. It is for this reason that financial incentives are now been offered by the regulatory authorities in the United States to whistle-blowers for information that leads to a conviction. Many argue that the same is needed in the United Kingdom and elsewhere.

We also saw in Chapter 9 that a system is a mental construct. It is not tangible or real but instead given by what actually holds particular people and activities together at a particular point in time and is, therefore, moveable and changeable. So while a board and its members might exist, as a box, at the top of an organizational chart and look like a working group, the risk is that it is not. Take AIG, one of the case studies that I referred to in Chapter 2. There, Hank Greenberg, the long-standing CEO, who to call charismatic is an understatement, handpicked the board members during the years when he was the dominating CEO. His board comprised simply two types: loyal friends and colleagues who would leave his decisions unchallenged and support him regardless; and distinguished former politicians and government officials chosen 'to add prestige to the board'. This weakened the board by creating dual systems with different purposes and therefore tasks. Board members had to make decisions in their role based on the actual system that they were part of and its unique purpose. This meant that they could not then do the primary work of the board which was, in part, to provide the checks and balances required to stop Greenberg from destroying the company. The result was that AIG subsequently lost its AA rating. Five people were jailed for conspiracy and fraud and Greenberg paid $15 million to the US Securities and Exchange Commission.

Whole and part

We looked at systemic thinking in Chapter 8 and how the whole reflects the parts and vice versa. This means that patterns of behaviour exhibited by the board will be replicated elsewhere and anything done within this sub-system, for better or worse, will impact and affect the whole. It follows that board members need to be acutely aware of the impact that their own behaviours will have on the system as a whole. A charismatic CEO like Hank Greenberg may have been enamoured by his own hubris but where did that get AIG in the end?

Stated values or mission statements are of little use here when the behaviours actually demonstrate something else. For example, at Independent Insurance, if other values were stated, the message from those around the CEO Michael Bright was to be complicit in his concealing the true level of reserves. Most people complied or left without raising the alarm. The values, as stated on the last annual accounts for Enron, included 'integrity' and 'respect'. So how board members behave and what they pay attention to will become a microcosm for the rest of the organization with patterns of behaviour adopted there replicated elsewhere in the system. Boards set the tone.

The flow can work in a number of different directions and perhaps the French bank Société Générale provides a good example. In January 2008, the bank discovered that a rogue trader, Jérôme Kerviel, had lost an amount eventually determined to be nearly €5 billion. The board should not really have been surprised about the possibility of their harbouring a 'rogue trader' because between Nick Leeson (who brought Barings down in 1995) and 2008, the activities of at least seven other major rogue traders had been uncovered – roughly one every two years. The compliance team had noticed irregularities in Kerviel's trading but proved powerless to stop it. Perhaps, the status of the traders system was greater in the eyes of the board than that of compliance but certainly each sub-system was operating ineffectually as part of the whole.

Context

Working from the outside in is becoming an ever more critical skill for a board because survival is that much more assured if an organization stays fully connected and knows then how best to respond to the demands of their operating environment. It is also a critical skill because if organizational purpose is defined from outside the organization as well as within, then it needs discovering and rediscovering as the context invariably changes.

Boards then need to learn to see the whole, system as well as context, and to keep that vigilant awareness with them at all times. We saw some obvious examples of this with Kodak, Sony, Apple, Amazon and Starbucks in earlier chapters. There are also organizations with high ideals where the founder has developed a particular and unique product that might be helped by this approach. Say, for example, the 5Rhythms organization, which provides a meditation dance system in the United States. Its founder, Gabrielle Roth, who developed the practice and trained thousands of people in the work died, leaving the intellectual property rights to her son. However, other people who had been significantly involved with Roth in developing and delivering the work prior to this may also feel a need and an entitlement to help govern the product after her death. This can often lead to splits within a community that was, prior to this point, fully behind the work. The organization can then become weakened by those splits, leading to varying and diluted versions of the product being offered by individual and unconnected practitioners. But what if the question were asked from the outside in? What if with non-attachment and non-desire, practitioners were to ask what does the world want and need from this product or gift right now? What then would that tell them about purpose and hence the right constitution for the board? What might then need to be let go of by those who had assumed entitlement, legal or otherwise, and in order for the work to flourish in the world. Perhaps, working in this way a stronger product offering could emerge because people, who might otherwise have left, can instead take up a role meaningfully on behalf of the whole system and in the service of context. Working from the outside in can, therefore, help us to remember a point that I made in Chapter 6 about none of this being personal, even if it feels excruciatingly personal and indeed painful at times.

Barriers to enlightenment

As I said above, board members are responsible for applying the two-pronged approach and doing the work outlined in Parts 2 and 3 of this book. That accountability includes being on the lookout for the kinds of defensive patterns of behaviour that I have outlined in Chapters 4 and 7. Some of these potential risk areas are outlined below.

Repression

We all repress. It is our nature and a primal attempt to avoid pain. The only cure is to develop more consciousness and try to lift the veils of awareness so that more of what we choose, at some unconscious level, not to see can be revealed to us. That means that as board members we must first do this work on our own behalf. Then as a group we must implement some of the practices outlined in Chapter 7 and at a minimum use Exercise 7.4, Double Task, as an operating framework so that attention is always being paid to the task as well as the process of the board.

Failing that the board will exist in a rose-tinted bubble with things that it could or should have known becoming unmanaged risks. The Roads to Ruin research found that 'Boards, and particularly Chairmen and NEDs [Non-Executive Directors], can have a large blind spot in this dangerous area. Without board leadership, these risks will remain hidden because only boards have the power to ensure that enough light is shed on those hard-to-see risks.'

Denial

Where do I start? Certainly 'It's not happening' seemed to have been the reactive response of many of the boards in the Roads to Ruin case studies. Just look at the examples of Société Générale and Independent Insurance above.

This risk will remain unless and until board members wake up. Until then, there needs to be people on the board with the skills and experience necessary to question corporate strategy and senior management styles in an effective way. This will only happen if the role and status of organizational development practitioners and other risk professionals is elevated so that they can confidently report and discuss all that they find on these subjects at all levels including, if not more especially, the board. The old hierarchical organizational model militated against this in practice. Hopefully, now, the newer, flatter networked reality will enable it to occur.

I was recently asked to attend a Tomorrow's Company board governance forum where Anthony Fry, Chairman of the UK Premier League, was asked if he thought that boards could use the services of an organizational psychologist. His answer was 'Yes I think an hour with an organizational psychologist would be helpful for board members'. I am of the view that unless and until board members wake up, by doing the work in Parts 2 and 3 of this book, an organizational psychologist might be essential *on* the board in order to help safeguard it against the risks brought about by denial.

Splitting

Splitting is rife; for example, the split board described above that was created by Hank Greenberg, the CEO of Independent Insurance. There is a practice too of putting work that is required by the organization as a whole into one part of the system and in that way splitting it off. This often happens with learning and development where, for example, a board might approve a leadership programme for a certain level of management which is designed to promote courageous conversations and then does little to improve its own dialogue at the top, thereby weakening the overall impact of the work on the whole system.

Sometimes too, a board will act as if it is the role of the non-executive directors to challenge it, thereby making the assumption that everyone else can carry on in their usual unenquiring manner and so weakening the overall level of debate and curiosity throughout.

Projection

Projection is one of the major obstacles to developing a real relationship with other board members and particularly those with power such as the Chair or CEO. It is one of the reasons that 'charismatic' leaders such as Hank Greenberg, Michael Bright and Ken Lay wreaked such havoc on their boards. Board members, perhaps, projected feelings of omnipotence and powerfulness unto them thus abdicating themselves from the responsibility of having to challenge or create dialogue and debate.

Again, this risk will remain, if board members do not do their own work here and, in practising the exercises outlined in Parts 2 and 3 of this book, learn to take back their own projections, see things as they really are and respond appropriately.

Introjection

Introjection is where a board member accepts feelings that are projected onto him or her, albeit unconscious of having done so. The recent Davies report in the UK recommends more women on boards to enable diversity and broader thinking. This all makes sense but some studies show that a minimum of three women might be required on any board for the women to be really effective in role. Certainly a 40 per cent quota was introduced some years ago in Norway. This sounds controversial, I know, and has nothing to do with a lack of competence in the women. It can, however, possibly be explained by the idea that a lone woman will suffer the projections of all the other male board members and, regardless of what these are, may find it very difficult not to introject them, acting as if they were then true.

The men may be actually delighted with their new talented female colleague – rationally, at least. Unconsciously, however, they might be asking her to carry the devalued parts of themselves, such as their feelings of impotence in 'not knowing'.

The work then would be for her to recognize when she is acting and feeling in ways that are not her own, questioning why. Perhaps she notices that her comments are not being heard and that she is beginning to contribute less. The work for the men is to begin to see how they are treating her and to face the parts of themselves that they are disowning. This all takes courage and grace, to accept ourselves and the other with all our human fragility and potentiality, but at the end of the day it is a choice: between effectiveness and ineffectiveness.

Systems thinking supports this idea by requiring us to view ourselves and others, not as isolates in a social vacuum, but rather as interdependent creatures, in part governed and unconsciously and inextricably bound together into a collective entity. It, helpfully, highlights the power that any group can have, with its shared patterns of projection and introjection, to shape and control your role and contributions, for better or worse. That is, if you choose to let it.

Competition

Competition has a very different place in the new organizational reality where collaboration and the building of trust is key. Yes, organizations must compete in the sense of flourishing and making their mark in the world but boards need to be mindful of the need to build strong relationships and to engender trust and collaboration. The Roads to Resilience research highlights this shift, finding that the more successful and resilient companies had boards that promoted an integral approach; recognizing that no one individual, no one function and no one organization is as smart as many thinking together. These organizations had built a significant radar across many boundaries and could then respond to their context swiftly and appropriately. They valued and rewarded shared learning as well as transparency.

Narcissism

Narcissism is closely related to competition and a sense of being right, the saviour or the chosen one. It is all about me, me and me. The latest experience that I have had of this was the head of a local school, who having perhaps overstayed her years, came to see the school more as an extension of herself. Curiously, it is managing perfectly well since her retirement. In the corporate world, too, there is often a lot of hubris about the importance of its executives, as if they are somehow special and their generation different. So too in academia, where 'brand me' stands in the way of true collaboration.

This is because there is a very real tendency for those in power to think that success is all their doing. Nicholas Taleb (2005) perceptively explains that successful leaders can be fooled into thinking that their success is due to their skills rather than good luck or a myriad of other factors. So boards need to always question their success or risk falling into the trap that AIG, Enron and Independent Insurance all did of believing quarterly results that were just too good to be true.

Pleasing

Pleasing is a death knell to challenge and debate. It is about seeking approval from the group at the expense of authentic self-expression. It is a critical impairment to board performance in limiting, for example, the NED from asking the challenging questions, the woman representing diversity from making her real contribution, the headhunter from putting forward someone suitably different for the post and maybe even stopping the board from being more requiring of its leaders and managers.

Collusion

Collusion, otherwise known as groupthink, is where members have become, all or some, stuck together and inculcated in a similar pattern of thinking. They are no longer asking individually what is required of them in role for the benefit of the whole. Collusion relieves them of accountability for decision making and is an abdication of their individual fiduciary duty of care as board members. I have too many examples to cite of where this has happened in practice. Instead, I caution you of the need to be vigilant against this tendency for groupthink to overtake all or part of the board. You must, instead, try to remain separate in your role and practice the disciplines set out in this book so that you can build your skill of being able to see more clearly what is actually going on and then take steps to transform it.

Collusion is the antithesis of diversity and inclusion, aspects that are core to the new organizational reality and which mean exploring, learning from and including differences. The real risk for boards is that they can never embrace diversity and real inclusion if they cannot themselves, as a group, get over collusion and this they cannot do without having the skills and commitment to challenge and debate. Conflict is an enormous resource anywhere in an organization but especially at board level. It follows that the courageous conversation framework outlined in Chapter 6 can be of enormous help to a board in safeguarding it against this risk.

Pairing

Pairing is altogether natural and common: preferring one board member over another or being attached to someone because they helped you into the role. However, it is always important to remember that the role is not personal but professional and your job is to concern yourself only with the long-term performance of the organization and fulfilling your particular role to the best of your ability. Watch if any pairing is getting in the way of that. Yours or another's.

Sabotage and scapegoating

These are outlined in Chapter 7 and apply to any board as much as any other working group. It follows that attention must also be applied to see if these are playing out and impacting on performance.

Ways through the barriers

Progress on any board can only be achieved if members acknowledge these defensive patterns of behaviour and engage with the reality of what is actually occurring between them. This means members doing their own work in noticing and then taking back their projections and defensive patterns of response. It means them working more consciously in role and to purpose. At the level of the group, it means building in practices and supports, such as the double task and courageous conversations frameworks, that will enable the board to develop more awareness and competence about itself as a sub-system and thereby also set a tone from the top that resonates throughout the rest of the organization and beyond.

The enlightened organization

To conclude, the enlightened organization is the one that chooses to see clearly, to be real and to face and be with the actuality of what is happening to it right here and right now. It plays with time, encompassing the past as well as the future, while remaining firmly rooted in the present. It plays with space by extending its view beyond its boundaries to see what is occurring both within and without. But fundamentally it is its deep understanding and compassion for what it means to be human that distinguishes it from others, knowing that in many ways, like for all of us, enlightenment is more about a direction of travel than any final destination.

The privilege of the role

Governance is, in my view, about playing a part in helping to create the enlightened organization. It is a privilege and an honour to be trusted with the role and, as with being a parent or other caretaker, there can be almost insurmountable joy in seeing the 'baby' develop and grow.

Those of us who take on the role, wherever that might be within the organization, need to be responsible and accountable accordingly. As Khalil Gibran says, our 'children' are not our own. They are 'Life's longing for itself'. You are the bows from which they 'as living arrows are sent forth'. I leave you then with Gibran's line: 'Let your bending in the archer's hand be for gladness; For even as he loves the arrow that flies, so He loves also the bow that is stable.'

KEY POINTS

1 Governance is about directing the longer-term performance of the organization and those who take on the role become accountable for doing this to the best of their ability. In some cases, they owe a fiduciary duty of care to key stakeholders.

2 Board members need to attend to the work required by a two-pronged approach. They need to investigate the personal and interpersonal as well as the system and context, without preference for one over the other and at all times balancing and fine-tuning elements within each. In short, this means their doing the work required within Parts 2 and 3 of this book.

3 The Grounding Steps framework can help a board to navigate its way through changing and unknown waters. It can root a board in its purpose and core strengths while also enabling it to remain open, flexible and responsive. Ultimately, if applied, it can enable a board to discern the better path to follow and to make explicit and conscious choices about the steps that its organization needs to take in order to better embrace the challenges and opportunities that lie before it.

4 The Integral model, as an overarching systemic framework, can help a board to keep its organization in a balanced and optimal state of health.

5 The Context model will enable a board to stay connected with the operating environment, answering the bigger strategic questions about the organization from the outside in.

6 Board members and everyone else acting in role on behalf of the organization needs to make a conscious choice about whether they want to be able to see or not; to see what is really going on so that they can help their organization respond appropriately.

7 The role is a privileged one and worth the work required in that it will help realize an enlightened organization; setting it forth into the world, 'swift and far'.

LIBRARY, UNIVERSITY OF CHESTER

REFERENCES

Bazalgette, J, Irvine, B and Quine, C (2006) *The Purpose of Meaning and the Meaning of Purpose*, Paper delivered at the ISPSO conference. Available from the Grubb Institute, London

Belbin, M (1981) *Management Teams: Why they succeed or fail*, Heinemann, London

Bion, W B (1955) Language and the schizophrenic, in *New Directions in Psychoanalysis*, ed M Klein, P Heimann and R Money-Kyrle, pp 220–39, Tavistock Publications, London

Bradford, L, Gibb, R and Benne, K (1964) *T-Group Theory and Laboratory Method*, Wiley, New York

Bridger, H, Main T F and Bion, W R (1946) The Northfield experiment. *Bulletin of the Menninger Clinic*, 1 (10), pp 71–76

Cameron, J (1992) *The Artist's Way: A course in discovering and recovering your creative self*, Putnam, New York

Cass Business School report on behalf of Airmic (2011) *Roads to Ruin: A study of major risk events: their origins, impacts and implications*

Cranfield School of Management executive briefing report on behalf of Airmic (2013) *Roads to Resilience: Building dynamic approaches to risk: protecting and championing trusted reputations in complex and uncertain business environments*

De Board, R (1978) *The Psychoanalysis of Organizations: A psychoanalytic approach to behaviour in groups and organizations*, Routledge, New York

De Bono, E (1985) *Six Thinking Hats*, Little Brown, Boston

Depue, R A and Morrone-Strupinsky, J V (2005) A neurobehavioral model of affiliative bonding: implications for conceptualizing a human trait of affiliation, *Behavioral and Brain Sciences*, 28, pp 131–350

Elliott, J and Clement, S (1991) *Executive Leadership: A practical guide to managing complexity,* Cason Hall & Co Publishers Ltd, Arlington VA

Foulkes, S and Anthony, J (1965) *Group Psychotherapy: The psychoanalytic approach*, Penguin, London

Frankyl, V (1959) *Man's Search For Meaning: The classic tribute to hope from the Holocaust,* Rider, London

Gilbert, P and Choden (2013) *Mindful Compassion*, Constable and Robinson, London

Handy, C (1986) *The Age of Unreason: New thinking for a new world*, Random House, London

Heffernan, M (2011) *Willful Blindness: Why we ignore the obvious at our peril*, Walker & Company, London

Heifetz, R (2009) *The Practice of Adaptive Leadership: Tools and tactics for changing your organization*, Harvard University Press, Boston

Hirschhorn, L (1991) *Managing in the New Team Environment: Skills, tools, and methods*, Addison-Wesley Publishing Co, Reading, Massachusetts

Keats, J (1817) Letters to George and Thomas Keats on 12th December 1817, England

Kegan, R and Lahey, L (2009) *Immunity to Change: How to overcome it and unlock the potential in yourself and your organization*, Harvard Business Press, Boston

Kübler-Ross, E (1969) *On Death and Dying*, Simon and Schuster/ Touchstone, New York

LeDoux, J (1998) *The Emotional Brain: The mysterious underpinnings of emotional life*, Simon and Schuster, New York

Nadler, D and Tushman, L (1997) *Competing by Design: The power of organizational architecture*, Oxford University Press, Oxford

Panksepp, J (1998) *Affective Neuroscience: The foundations of human and animal emotions*, Oxford University Press, Oxford

Roberts, V and Bazalgette, J (2006) *Daring to Desire: Ambition, competition and role-transformation in 'idealistic' organizations*, Paper delivered at the ISPSO conference. Available from the Grubb Institute, London

Satir, V (1978) *Your Many Faces: The first step to being loved*, Souvenir Press, London

Scharmer, O (2009) *Theory U: Leading from the future as it emerges*, Berrett-Koehler Publishers, Inc, San Francisco

Senge, P, Scharmer, O and others (2005) *Presence: An exploration of profound change in people, organizations and society*, Nicholas Brealey Publishing, London

Stacey, R (1993) *Strategic Management and Organizational Dynamics: The challenge of complexity*, Pearson Education, Harlow

Suzuki, S (1970) *Zen Mind: Beginner's mind,* Shambhala Publications Inc, Boston

Taleb, N (2005) *Fooled by Randomness: The hidden role of chance in life and in the markets*, Random House, London

Thich Nhat Hanh (1991) *Peace Is Every Step: The path of mindfulness in everyday life*, Rider, London

Tolle, E (1999) *The Power of Now*, Hodder & Stoughton, London

Tomorrow's Good Governance Forum (2012) *Tomorrow's Corporate Governance: Improving the quality of boardroom conversations,* Centre for Tomorrow's Company, London

Tomorrow's Good Governance Forum (2013) *Tomorrow's Corporate Governance: The boardroom and risk,* Centre for Tomorrow's Company, London

Tuckman, B (1965) Developmental sequence in small groups, *Psychological Bulletin,* **63** (6), pp 384–99

Wheatley, Margaret (1993) *Leadership and the New Science: Discovering order in a chaotic world,* Berrett-Koehler, San Francisco

Wilbur, K (1996) *A Brief History of Everything,* Gill and Macmillan, Dublin

INDEX

NB: key points for each chapter are indexed as 'key points of chapters on'
NB: page numbers in *italics* indicate Figures

Also available from Kogan Page

ISBN: 978 0 7494 7081 4 Paperback August 2014

Order online at www.koganpage.com

Find out more; visit www.koganpage.com and
sign up for offers and regular e-newsletters.

Also available from Kogan Page

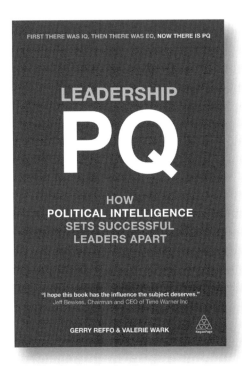

ISBN: 978 0 7494 6960 3 Paperback March 2014

Order online at www.koganpage.com

Find out more; visit www.koganpage.com and
sign up for offers and regular e-newsletters.

Also available from Kogan Page

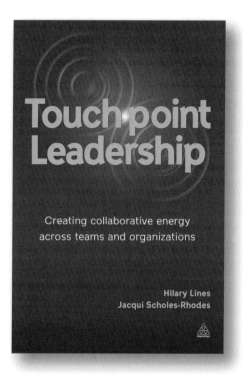

ISBN: 978 0 7494 6578 0 Paperback February 2013

Order online at www.koganpage.com

Find out more; visit www.koganpage.com and
sign up for offers and regular e-newsletters.

Also available from Kogan Page

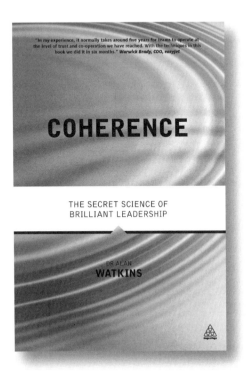

ISBN: 978 0 7494 7005 0 Paperback November 2013

Order online at www.koganpage.com

Find out more; visit www.koganpage.com and
sign up for offers and regular e-newsletters.